THE ORIGINS OF CANADIAN POLITICS

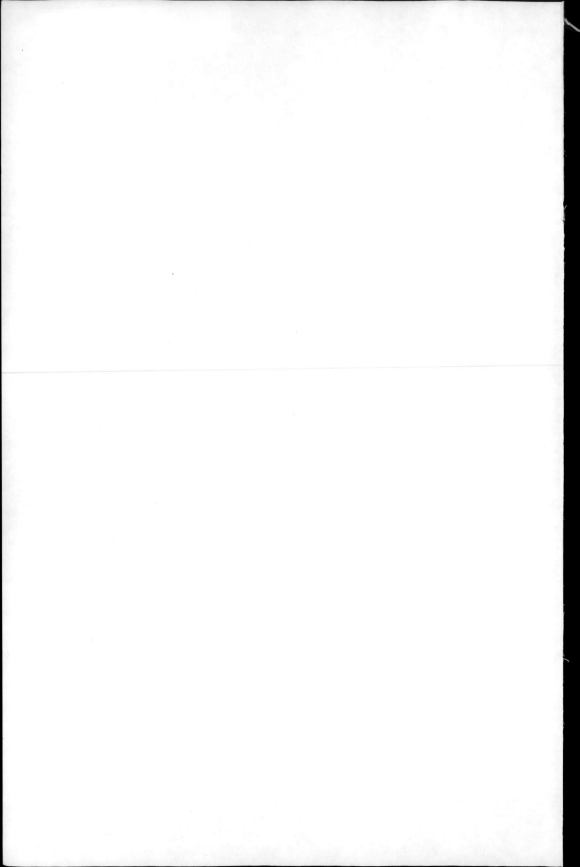

THE ORIGINS OF CANADIAN POLITICS
A Comparative Approach

Gordon T. Stewart

UNIVERSITY OF BRITISII COLUMBIA PRESS
VANCOUVER
1986

THE ORIGINS OF CANADIAN POLITICS
A COMPARATIVE APPROACH

This book has been published with the help of a grant from the Canadian Federation for the Humanities, using funds provided by the Social Sciences and Humanities Research Council of Canada.

Canadian Cataloguing in Publication Data

Stewart, Gordon T. (Gordon Thomas), 1945-
  The origins of Canadian politics

Bibliography: p.
Includes index.
ISBN 0-7748-0260-X

  1. Canada - Politics and government. 2. Comparative government.
I. Title. JL75.S84 1986   320.971   C86-091349-X

International Standard Book Number ISBN 0-7748-0260-X
Printed in Canada

CONTENTS

PREFACE

The need for a fresh look at the origins of Canadian politics struck me with some force as I examined, over the last five years or so, the papers of John A. Macdonald, Wilfrid Laurier, and their cabinet colleagues of the late nineteenth and early twentieth centuries. As I read the views and came to understand the assumptions and beliefs of these post-Confederation Canadian politicians on such matters as patronage deployment, the role of the prime minister, party leadership, and the nature of government power, I became convinced that what appeared to be a post-Confederation political culture had been largely moulded in the pre-1867 colonial period of Canadian history. While I knew the large body of scholarly work that traced aspects of the Canadian political tradition back to loyalist and pre-conquest French-Canadian sources (work that was initiated by Louis Hartz's approach to European settler societies like Canada and the United States as fragments of broader European cultures), I did not know of any sustained analysis that tried to assess how the working of politics during the entire colonial period from 1760 to 1867 created a distinctive and enduring pattern of Canadian politics.

The politics of the British colonial period tend to be viewed by post-Confederation historians and political scientists as parochial, personal, complex, and obscure (if occasionally dramatic), not easily susceptible to useful generalizations that can be applied to the entire subsequent sweep of Canadian history. The more I read in the Macdonald and Laurier papers, the more I thought about the matter, the more certain I became that this long formative stage of Canadian politics needed to be brought squarely into the analytical picture. The central question to be answered is a simple one — how did the workings of Canada's colonial political system lead to permanent characteristics of modern Canadian political culture?

From the outset I opted for a comparative approach to this question because comparison with Britain and America makes distinctive features of the colonial Canadian political landscape stand out in sharper relief. An internal recounting of politics in Upper and Lower Canada would merely have repeated a whole school of authoritative Canadian scholarship. I did not wish to repeat or summarize that but rather to concentrate on identifying those trends that were influential in the Canadas and which set Canadian politics apart from British or American politics in the eighteenth and first half of the nineteenth century. In pursuing this comparative approach, I used the "court-country" description of the political spectrum partly because I started right back in the seventeenth century to get at the origins of the modern Anglo-American-Canadian political world but also because the "court-country" duality has been applied very successfully by John Murrin in his recent work comparing England and America from 1688 to the 1820's. By adopting and adapting Murrin's framework, I could take stock of where the Canadian colonies stood in relation to Britain and America in the very middle of the colonial period. This "court-country" concept may be permissible as a device for discussing seventeenth- and eighteenth-century British politics, but it does become an anachronism when applied to nineteenth-century politics in Canada. In the nineteenth century, the "court" orientation developed into a statist outlook by which administrations of the day deployed patronage and influence to shore up their positions, stimulated and participated in economic growth, and tried to free themselves as much as possible from close legislative supervision; the "country" tradition by this date implied an emphasis on elective rather than appointive officialdom, a desire to make executives more controllable by legislatures, and a penchant for small government frequently answerable to the electorate. In the course of my analysis, I begin to substitute statist for "court" or use the two in tandem after the 1840's. However, right to the end, I continue to use "court" as a heuristic device so the reader can fully appreciate how trends identified from the late eighteenth century were continued in various guises into post-Confederation Canada. I am not making an idiosyncratic effort to stretch the already over-long life of the "court-country" concept beyond its legitimate historical period but simply drawing attention, by use of this arresting anachronism, to the historical origins of the statist tradition in Canada at both the federal and provincial levels.

In concentrating on such themes as patronage, power, and influence, I may appear cynical to some readers. It is essential to understand that my object is limited to answering the particular question posed above. This does not mean that I think Canadian politicians of the colonial and post-Confederation periods were selfish men seeking only to improve their own and their parties' welfare. All of them thought that what they were doing was in the best interests of the colony, province, or federation. This is as true for the Tory ruling groups in the pre-1837 Canadas as for Macdonald and Laurier after Confederation. These politicians had ideas about economic growth, about Canada's place in North America, and about her role in the British Empire. Some of them even had ideals about the nature of the good society. All of them tried hard to ameliorate Canada's complex ethnic and religious tensions. In short, like most politicians, they were a mixture of selfishness and idealism, busily building their own careers and parties while striving to serve the public interest. I hardly deal at all with this ideological dimension, but those readers who are not well read on this well-worn topic can turn to such introductions as William Christian and Colin Campbell, *Political Parties and Political Ideologies in Canada* or, for a full dose of idealism, to Donald Creighton's ever readable biography of Canada's greatest politician, *John A. Macdonald.* A more recent account that complements this study even better because it offers an empirical check on all those general and theoretical comparisons of Canadian and American political cultures going back to loyalist times, is Roger Gibbons and Neil Neville, "Canadian Political Ideology: a Comparative Approach," *Canadian Journal of Political Science* 18 (1985):577-98.

If this book eschews conventional political ideology, it sins in perhaps an even more shameful fashion for these days because it appears to neglect social history. In this view of things, it is old-fashioned; it concentrates on high politics. I have no defence against such a charge — it is true. However, it is most important to notice that I do relate political developments to the material conditions in Canada between the 1790's and 1910 by outlining how economic and social conditions provided a favourable setting within which certain political tendencies could flourish. I hasten to add that I have nothing against social history. On the contrary, my own earlier work on religious revivalism in late eighteenth-century Nova Scotia was solidly within that field, consisting as it did, in its later stages, of a detailed community study of Yarmouth to uncover connections between wealth, property, social status, and response to evangelical religion. I did not take such an approach in this analysis of the origins of Canadian politics simply because I was trying to answer different kinds of questions. Much of the best and most stimulating recent work in Canada is being done in the field of social history, and my concentration on high politics is not a statement about the value of a particular kind of history writing. Surely the one great strength of the discipline of history is that it allows for a variety of approaches to the study of the past. There is a tendency among contemporary historians in Canada to cleave even more strongly to social history and its ramifications because of a widespread belief that all the great political history writing of the past two generations of scholarship has answered all the big questions. It has not.

I wish to acknowledge the support and encouragement I received from several quarters in the preparation and writing of this book. The staff at the Public Archives of Canada was characteristically welcoming and helpful. Here at Michigan State University, Professor Victor Howard has been a pillar of strength not only for me personally as a teacher and scholar but also for the Canadian Studies Program as a whole. My conversations with my colleague Dr. William Hixson on American and comparative politics were always illuminating. At an early stage of the work, I received much needed advice from Professor Jack Granatstein (then editor of the *Canadian Historical Review*) and Professor Keith Johnson of Carleton University in Ottawa. Direct encouragement at a critical stage when my spirits were flagging came from Professors Peter Ward and R.K. Carty of the University of British Columbia. It is especially important with a book like this, which proposes a comprehensive new thesis about the origins of Canadian politics, to absolve these people of any complicity in errors of fact or interpretation.

CHRONOLOGY

1608-1759	Canada a French colony.
1759-60	British military conquest of Canada.
1763	Canada formally ceded to Britain by Treaty of Paris.
1774	Quebec Act organizes colonial government with a governor and appointed council but no assembly.
1783-84	Loyalist migration to Quebec, most settling in pockets along the north shore of the St. Lawrence and the lakes west of Montreal.
1791	Canada Act of Pitt's administration divides Quebec into two separate colonies — Upper Canada and Lower Canada. Each colony had a governor (lieutenant-governor in Upper Canada), appointed executive and legislative councils and assemblies. These two colonies evolved into the modern provinces of Quebec (Lower Canada) and Ontario (Upper Canada).
1800-1828	Political struggles in both Lower and Upper Canada between opposition in assemblies and the executive.
1828-37	Political struggle becomes more intense as Reformers, hoping for support from Whig governments in London, increase pressure on Tory ruling groups. These groups are called by

	the Reform opposition the Family Compact (Upper Canada) and the Chateau Clique (Lower Canada).
1837	Rebellions in Lower and Upper Canada. In Lower Canada the leader was Louis-Joseph Papineau; in Upper Canada, William Lyon Mackenzie. Both rebellions failed partly because of lack of effective military leadership by these two men but also because of insufficient popular support.
1838-39	Lord Durham sent over by British government to investigate and report on conditions in Canada
1840-41	Upper and Lower Canada reunited into one colony called the Union of the Canadas (1841-67). Upper Canada becomes Canada West; Lower Canada becomes Canada East. Same constitutional system kept in place: — governor, appointed executive council, appointed legislative council and elected assembly.
1841-49	Bitter political struggle between Reform party in Union Assembly and the governors with their Tory and Conservative party supporters. Reformers led by Louis-Hippolyte LaFontaine from Canada East and Robert Baldwin from Canada West. Reform leaders fight to enforce their version of Durham's "responsible government" — that is, to make governor choose as his advisors those politicians who commanded a majority in the assembly.
1844	A critical year when the political battle comes to a head. Governor Metcalfe clashes with LaFontaine and Baldwin over control of government patronage.
1847-54	Governorship of Lord Elgin, during which responsible government is conceded as Elgin allows full reign to Baldwin and LaFontaine to run the administration and control patronage.
1849	Outraged Tory mob riots in Montreal and burns down Parliament Buildings.
1851	LaFontaine and Baldwin leave active politics believing their goals have been achieved.

1851-54   Political realignment as old Reform party breaks up on religious and other policy issues. Former French Canadian Reformers now join with English Canadian Tories and Conservatives and some moderate Reformers to create a new party. Initially styled the Liberal-Conservative party it became the Conservative party and held power for most of the next forty years both in the Union and in the post-1867 Confederation. On the Reform side two rumps were left — the small liberal group in Montreal, called the *rouges* and a much more numerous following especially strong in the western districts beyond Toronto, called the Grits. The *rouges* and the Grits formed the basis of the Liberal party in post-Confederation Canada.

1854-64   Union political and government system becomes deadlocked. Administrations found it difficult to manage the assembly and pressure built up against system in Canada West because English Canadians believed the Union was being dominated by French Canadians. (Seats in the Assembly were equally divided between Canada East and Canada West but by 1850's Canada West's English-speaking population had outstripped population in Canada East)

1867   Union of the Canadas dissolved and the British North America Act creates the Dominion of Canada. The new confederation has four provinces—Quebec, Ontario (the old Canadas), Nova Scotia and New Brunswick.

1867-96   Conservative party in power (except for 1874-78) John A. Macdonald prime minister 1867-73, 1878-91.

1870   Manitoba enters Confederation.

1871   British Columbia enters Confederation.

1873   Prince Edward Island enters Confederation.

1870-1905   Old Hudsons Bay Company lands organized as the Northwest Territories.

1905   Alberta and Saskatchewan become provinces.

1896-1911   Liberal party in power. Wilfrid Laurier as prime minister.

INTRODUCTION

The purpose of this work is to explain when and why Canadian political culture diverged from British and American patterns. All three polities stem from a similar constitutional and institutional background in the eighteenth century, but each ended up by the middle of the nineteenth century with its own sharply differentiated political system. In the case of the United States, the critical changes came during the revolutionary and constitution-making period from the 1760's to the 1790's, during which British and colonial institutions, concepts and practices were transformed into new republican forms. The corresponding formative period for Canadian political development was from the 1790's to the 1840's. Beginning in 1791 with local constitutions similar to those of the former royal colonies in America (governor, appointed executive and legislative councils, representative assemblies) and with political values close to those of the late-eighteenth, early-nineteenth century British setting (acceptance of a narrow governing class and an official church, a limited reach of politics into society, a partial representative check by an assembly on ministerial authority), the Canadian colonies by the 1850's had arrived at a political culture quite different from those in monarchical Britain and republican America. There were in place by the 1850's specifically Canadian concepts of the monarchical constitution, of executive power, of party politics, and the nature and style of party leadership. This political culture was clearly quite a different beast from the republican and democratic American polity, but British observers in the 1850's and 1860's, more surprisingly, were struck by how different it was from parties and politics in Victorian Britain. An explanation of this great Canadian divergence from American and British paths provides the focal point of this study.

The case made is a companion-piece to the work done by Bernard Bailyn.

In his seminal study, *The Origins of American Politics,*[1] Bailyn explained how conditions in the American colonies allowed the British-appointed governors too little patronage and influence to enable them to "manage" the colonial assemblies. In eighteenth-century Britain the executive (the ministers chosen by the Crown) depended on patronage and influence to maintain support in Parliament and run the king's government. In spite of all the cant about the balanced constitution with Crown, Lords, and Commons acting in distinct capacities, the eighteenth-century British constitution worked because there was a complex intermixing of ministers and members of Parliament. In the North American colonies, however, the local versions of the royal executive were not able to exercise similar influence because they did not control a sufficient number of jobs or large enough discretionary revenues. As a consequence, the colonial assemblies were able to protect their autonomy and build up their power to the point where most governors were isolated politically, weak in terms of their ability to wield wide-ranging executive influence, and typically ineffective in their efforts to manage the assemblies.[2] It was part of British policy in the 1763 to 1776 period (so the American patriots were convinced) to reverse these trends and shore up the governors by providing revenues and jobs (especially in the customs service) free of assembly control. Although the working of politics varied in each colony depending on the configuration of local circumstances, Bailyn has made the cardinal point that these patterns of political behavior set up in America, long before the advent of independence and self-conscious republicanism, a political culture in which the executive and the legislature operated in discrete, contending spheres.

   Bailyn's carefully elaborated insight that major characteristics of American politics had their roots in the British colonial period has been nicely complemented by John Murrin in his comparative study of political development in England after the 1688 revolution and in America after the 1776 revolution.[3] In one of the most ingenious and satisfying recent pieces of scholarship on the Anglo-American political world of the eighteenth-century, Murrin has drawn out the full significance of the strikingly different outcomes of these two British revolutions, notwithstanding the similarities of their rhetoric at the outset. In England by the 1720's, the "court" Whigs were controlling, in collaboration with George I, a national government that routinely influenced Parliament, that manipulated elections, that was part of a complex central banking and fiscal system, and that in the course of the wars with France between 1689 and 1713 had built Europe's most powerful navy. This was a far cry from the "country" rhetoric the Whigs had used in 1688 to criticize the centralizing or absolutist policies of James II. The radical "country" case of 1688 had dissolved into a vindication of strong national government. Mainstream whiggery was transformed into justification of an aristocratic, oligarchic ruling elite. In the class structure of

England, politics was largely the preserve of the aristocracy and the landed gentry, and there was acceptance of a natural ruling class. This, coupled with the fact that the revitalized national government pointedly left local county government alone, permitted the transition to take place without much soul-searching among the Whig politicians who ran and benefited from the system. The danger of an absolute monarchy may have been averted when James II was forced off the throne, but in its place there emerged a system of strong national government.

In contrast to the 1688 revolutionary settlement in England, the American revolution ended up by the 1820's with a very weak form of central government. The intensity and popularity of republican ideology, the power of the state legislatures and suspicion of gubernatorial power inherited from the colonial period, the lack of demographic homogeneity in the new country, the instability produced by territorial and population expansion, the more democratic setting of politics and the failure of the Federalists to impose their concept of a national ruling class, all these weakened the weight and reach of national government in the United States. Influential crown government able to manage Parliament had resulted from revolution in England; small central government with a tenuous influence on the legislature and the states had resulted from the American revolution. The federal government in the United States "remained minuscule, a midget institution in a giant land."[4]

The Canadian case presents an interesting third option to the lines of development taken in Britain and the United States. Looking at the surface of things, the Canadian colonies should have followed one or the other of these two major precedents. On the one hand, British policy ever since the conquest of Canada in 1759-60 had been to establish a strong executive in Canada. Even after William Pitt's Canada Act of 1791 gave each of the two Canadian colonies (Upper and Lower Canada) an elected assembly, the local constitutions were so arranged that the executive would remain dominant over assemblies circumscribed in their abilities to raise and appropriate revenue. British policy-making from 1760 to the 1790's in Canada would seem, then, to have guaranteed the emergence of strong crown government on the British model. Yet, on the other hand, in spite of British expectations, a political pattern quickly asserted itself between the 1790's and 1830's that bore remarkable similarities to the political culture of the American colonies. As the local economy and population grew, the assemblies in Upper and Lower Canada began organized attacks on the privileged and exclusive executives. Canadian politics appeared to be settling into the contentious mode that Bailyn saw as the beginnings of American politics.

Thus, between 1760 and the 1830's, conditions in the Canadas seemed to presage a repetition of either the British or American courses. But neither of these pre-existing paths was followed. Instead, a peculiar hybrid political culture, a distinctively "Canadian" politics, emerged by the 1840's and

1850's. In Britain and the United States the great constitutional issues that set the parameters of the political game had been long settled, but in Canada between the 1790's and 1850's, there was a prolonged struggle between British values and institutions and North American and Canadian conditions, a struggle that made Canadian political culture complex and difficult to define, a struggle that prevented a clear-cut British or American definition of politics from emerging.

Insofar as a beginning has already been made on the Canadian definition of politics from a comparative perspective, it stems from the writings of Louis Hartz on the new settler societies created by European expansion. In his *Founding of New Societies* and *The Liberal Tradition in America*, Hartz and scholarly collaborators from other countries made the case that all European settler cultures were fragments from the more extended spectrum of European societies.[5] The way in which political culture developed in each colony depended to a large extent on the characteristics of the original fragment that came from Europe and on the nature and timing of the fragment's final break from European control and influence. In the application of these concepts to Canada, a leading role was taken by Gad Horowitz, who focused attention on the Loyalists from the Thirteen Colonies as the first major English settler group to mould concepts of society, government, and politics.[6] According to this line of argument, the Loyalists brought with them a cluster of conservative values and concepts. They accepted hierarchy in society, they believed that deference was the cement of society, and they believed in monarchical government with an appointed executive. This conservative tradition marked off Canada from the United States which, now cleared of its last tinge of old-world values, proceeded down its liberal, anti-statist path. The Loyalist migration preserved in Canada what was missing in the restricted American setting—a dialectic between left and right. For, so the argument runs, the legitimacy of the conservative view of an organic society over which the state has some kind of nurturing role enabled later opposition parties in Canada to take up statist positions without being disloyal to native political traditions. Put at its most extreme, the case is that loyalism in the late eighteenth century sanctioned the emergence of a viable, legitimate socialism in the twentieth century.

The Hartz-Horowitz approach to understanding Canadian political culture is a valuable one and has provided the basis for much fruitful scholarly work.[7] Apart from Horowitz's early work and Kenneth McCrae's chapter on Canada in *The Founding of New Societies*, the most sophisticated effort so far to use the Hartzian model has been made by David Bell and Lorne Tepperman in *The Roots of Disunity* (1979). The great strength of this book is that the authors actually try to trace how the original fragment values were passed on from generation to generation. It is very good on modern Canada, but the treatment of the 1760 to 1867 colonial period does not get beneath the surface of events. In so far as there is a weakness in this body of work, it is a tendency to assume that the original fragments were static and to ignore the complicating interplay of historical conditions and personalities. In the case of Canada, there is the additional problem that Canada is a two-fragment culture and that the Loyalist and French-Canadian fragments exerted separate and sometimes conflicting influences. These two fragments were brought into contact between 1783 and the 1840's. The task is to descend a bit from the theoretical level, to push from our minds preoccupations stemming from the current configuration of Canadian politics, in an effort to understand how these elements interacted. A more dynamic treatment of this early period of contact is needed to take into account more fully all the historical factors that were fermenting to produce the distinctive brew of Canadian politics.

The key to understanding the main features of Canadian national political culture after 1867 lies in the political world of Upper and Lower Canada between the 1790's and 1840's. The players in this political drama were the French-Canadian settlers, who had experienced a hundred years of authoritarian, non-representative monarchical rule; the Loyalists who had fled from the new American republic; American settlers who arrived later; the post-1815 immigrants from Britain; and the solidly entrenched governing elites in both Upper and Lower Canada. The political culture that would emerge from such a mix could have taken several directions, depending on social conditions and the balance of political forces within each colony. The ways in which other colonies within the British Empire developed (such as the Cape and Natal, New Zealand and the Australian colonies) demonstrate the variety of possible outcomes.[8] In all of these cases, the colonies shifted from Crown-controlled government to government in which the local executive was responsible to the elected assemblies. This was achieved as British governors appointed to their executive councils politicians who were able to control a majority in the assemblies. The distinguishing feature marking Canada as the odd-man out among all the British colonies that moved towards responsible government in the course of the nineteenth century was that responsible government came only after a prolonged, bitter, and violent struggle. The extraordinary divisive political battles lasted from the late 1820's to the late 1840's, including armed rebellions in 1837 and culminating in the destruction by burning of the Parliament Buildings in Montreal in 1849. Such persistent political violence had no parallel anywhere else in the post-1783 British Empire. Even the other British North American colonies that received responsible government in the 1840's, like Nova Scotia, were struck by the turmoil and violence in the Canadian political world.

This protracted and heated political epoch was the crucible within which

Canadian politics were moulded when Loyalist, French-Canadian, and British monarchical values were brought into a new relationship. It was this unique period of high political tension that made subsequent Canadian politics different from politics in other British colonies in the nineteenth century, even colonies as close as Nova Scotia. All these colonies went through similar constitutional changes in the middle decades of the century. In each, there was a shift from gubernatorial rule to party rule, a shift from metropolitan to local control, a change from oligarchic to more democratic politics. Yet no other colony experienced the turbulent, violent transition that occurred in Canada. That agonizing transformation left permanent features on the Canadian political landscape.

For readers who may be unfamiliar with the details of Canadian history, it will be useful at this point to set down an outline of Canadian history during this critical period. Following the conquest and acquisition of Canada during the Seven Years' War (1756-63), the British ran the newly acquired French colony of Quebec as a crown colony with a British governor and, following the Quebec Act of 1774, an appointed council. In 1791, the British reorganized this old colony of Quebec by splitting it into two separate colonies—Upper Canada (west of the Ottawa River) and Lower Canada (the French-Canadian heartland). This division was made necessary by the influx of thousands of Loyalists who, once they arrived in British territory, displayed deep misgivings about living under the constitutional and legal arrangements of the 1774 Act. Under the 1791 Canada Act, each colony was provided with a governor, appointed executive and legislative councils, and elected assemblies. It is important to understand that the Quebec Revenue Act (14 George III, c.83) of 1774 remained in effect, providing revenue based on customs duties and other Crown income to the governors.[9] In both colonies ruling elites were consolidated on the basis of the governors' patronage powers and the governors' ability to control revenue under the terms of the 1774 Act.

By 1800 in the case of Lower Canada and by the 1820's in Upper Canada, those excluded from the narrow governing circles began to organize opposition in the assemblies, an opposition which turned into armed rebellions in each colony in 1837. Although unsuccessful and not supported by a majority of the Reformers, these rebellions forced the British to re-evaluate their Canadian policy, and in 1840-41, they rejoined the colonies into the Union of the Canadas. The Union still maintained the existing constitutional structure, but between 1841 and 1849 a bitter political struggle between governor and assembly in Canada (along with political changes in Britain) produced a form of responsible government in which the governor ruled through an executive council composed of party leaders who could organize a majority in the assembly. Because of the complicated tensions between the two great ethnic blocs in the Union and the consequent difficulties in the unified legislature, the Union was dissolved in 1867 and Upper and Lower Canada entered the new Canadian Confederation (along with the colonies of Nova Scotia and New Brunswick) as the provinces of Ontario and Quebec.[10]

An explanation must be made for leaving out of the analysis the Maritime colonies which joined the Canadian Confederation in 1867 and the Western provinces which entered Confederation between 1870 and 1906 (Manitoba, British Columbia, Saskatchewan, and Alberta). Clearly these provinces and regions did affect the working of Canadian politics after 1867. Cabinets were constructed to accommodate Maritime and Western interests, parliamentary manoeuvring and alignments were affected by Maritime and Western representation, policies were introduced, rejected, or amended in response to the range of regional pressures and demands. The case made here, however, is that the Maritime and Western provinces, while they had an impact on post-1867 government formation and parliamentary alignments and while they certainly forced attention to particular issues, did not make a fundamental alteration in the political culture already established in the pre-1867 Canadas. Just as American political culture was moulded in the more populous and politically advanced colonies and states from Virginia to Massachusetts, so was Canadian political culture nurtured in the economically and demographically dominant central Canadian colonies. Before outraged residents and historians of Canada's regions complain they have been neglected yet again, let me say I have a deep respect for the regional approach to Canadian history (as every scholar who studies Canada must). Indeed, in the case of the Maritimes I have spent several absorbing years studying the religious and social history in Nova Scotia of the last half of the eighteenth century. On this matter Maritimers at least can console themselves, as they so often do, with the thought that the Canadians are to blame for everything.

In this context, it is essential to understand that this study is not intended to re-do Canadian scholarship on the period. It does not attempt to assess historiographical debates on the conquest, on the rise of the professional middle class in Quebec, on the place of economic factors in the causes of the 1837 rebellions, or on the other standard topics that are the stuff of monographic and article literature. This work, in fact, could not have been attempted without that body of scholarly literature which is so well synthesized in the various volumes of the Canadian Centenary Series. Like Bailyn's work on the origins of American politics, this book does not investigate and reappraise the political, economic, and social issues of the day but rather tries to identify and extract from the mass of chronological detail, the salient features of the emerging Canadian political culture. This analysis stands back from the writings of specialists to view the course of Canadian political development from a more general and comparative angle of vision.

It is time for such an enterprise. There have been many great scholarly achievements in the writing of Canadian history in the past fifty years. The volumes of the Centenary Series are permanent monuments to first-class archival research and thoughtful scholarly synthesis. But as Carl Berger has pointed out in *The Writing of Canadian History*, Canadian historical writing has been conducted within a nationalist framework, as historians have told and retold (with ever-increasing discrimination and sophistication) the story of Canada's growth and travails.[11] When H.J. Hanham, the historian of nineteenth-century Britain then teaching at Harvard, was asked by the *Canadian Historical Review* to take stock of Canadian history writing in the 1970's, he was struck by the fact that most Canadian historians seemed uninterested in writing for the international scholarly community.[12] The analysis presented here breaks that mould. It relies on all the meticulous work done by Canadian historians, but the approach is that of an outsider who has lived and studied in Canada but who has taught Canadian history only on the outer periphery in Scotland and the United States. The different angle of vision consists of viewing the origins of Canadian politics from a fresh, outside perspective to explain why Canada took a different route from Britain and the United States out of the common heritage of the eighteenth-century Anglo-American political world.

1

THE BACKGROUND:
ENGLAND, AMERICA AND CANADA
1688-1828

The great fact of Confederation in 1867 has tended to obscure the origins of Canadian political culture. But Canadian politics have much deeper roots than the Confederation experience. John A. Macdonald, for example, who was the major presence in the Canadian political world between 1867 and 1891 and who had a critically important influence on the nature of party, party leadership, and the concept of executive power in Canada, had been in Canadian politics for almost a quarter of a century before 1867. His most basic political values and assumptions were set long before Confederation was created. Insofar as he looked for ideological reference points outside Canada, he turned not to the England of Gladstone and Disraeli but to the constitutional world of Pitt the Younger and Edmund Burke.[1] The political and constitutional structures that emerged after 1867 had their origins in the unstable decades of the 1830's and 1840's, which, in turn, were given their contentious character by the peculiar constitutions established in Upper and Lower Canada by the 1791 Canada Act. It was during these years from 1791 to the 1840's that conditions in the Canadas produced a political culture that differed both from the British political world of the 1790-1850 years and from the American political world that had been changed by revolution into a new republic.

Canada and the United States share a British colonial background, and both countries have political roots in the British political and constitutional patterns that developed after 1688. In the case of the United States, the successful rebellion marked a decisive break from the British patterns. During the transforming years between 1763 and 1789, British and colonial institutions and practices were changed into American republican forms with a formal separation of executive and legislative branches mandated in a written constitution. In so making a separation of executive and legislative functions, the Americans were trying to solve a complex problem of the post-1688 British system, which, notwithstanding all the balanced constitution rhetoric, brought the Crown's ministers, the executive, into a close reciprocally influential relationship with Parliament. This was a state of affairs which radical critics in England, and American patriots, were convinced led too easily to undue executive influence in Parliament and thus to corruption and tyranny. In Canada, after 1791, as in the eighteenth-century Anglo-American setting, the heart of the political problem was how to arrange the relationship between executive and legislature. Canada made no such drastic modification of the British and colonial structures as did the United States, but Canada did develop yet another variant of British forms. The process was less dramatic than that in the new country to the south, but by the middle of the nineteenth century, it had resulted in a marked disjunction between Britain and Canada in the way power was exercised and political parties functioned and in how politics were conducted.

When the Canadas received their first British-style constitutions in 1791, contemporaries on both sides of the Atlantic thought that Canada would develop along British lines, complete with an established church and a hereditary upper chamber equivalent to the House of Lords.[2] By the 1850's, while the British connection was still cherished and Canadians talked proudly of their monarchical constitution, the Canadian political world could no longer be seen as "the image and transcript" of the British one. By the 1850's, British governors to Canada were immediately struck by the differences between Canada and Britain. On the surface, things seemed familiar, but parties and governments, as British observers like the Earl of Dufferin noticed in the 1870's, had become quite different.[3] The terminology of politics was similar, but the political and constitutional river had split into separate courses.

To understand fully the consequences of Canada's divergence from British and American paths, the context must be broadened and Canadian conditions after 1791 viewed against political and constitutional developments in England and America after 1688. In England, the mixed constitution that evolved under William III and Mary, Anne, and the Hanoverian kings created English assumptions about the nature of the state, the role of central government, and relations between executive and legislature. Different values and assumptions about power and representation developed in England's American colonies. By placing these British and American patterns, as they had worked out between 1688 and the 1820's, squarely into the analysis, it will be possible to take stock of the post-1791 situation in Canada and, by comparison, illuminate what was distinctive about the origins of Canadian politics.

Turning first to England, it is important to understand the paradoxical consequences of the 1688 revolution in terms of the "court" and "country" tensions of the late seventeenth century.[4] "Court" supporters believed in active central government by the king and his appointed secretaries and officials; they believed in a state church to complement government power and maintain social stability; they believed the political nation should consist of those notables who had status and influence at the royal court where lay the centre of power. The more self-conscious "court" spokesmen looked to the France of Louis XIV as a model state where the king had absolute authority and maintained a royal bureaucracy and a standing army and where royal power was not checked by any countervailing parliamentary claims. It was possible for "court" defenders to see themselves as enlightened modernists intent on promoting good, efficient government to improve the whole realm and to depict opponents as old-fashioned defenders of local and special liberties. Louis XIV's state could be viewed as the way of the future.

However, the "court" position was rarely as clear-cut as this. James II, for example, as part of his plan to re-introduce Catholicism as a major influence in England, was prepared to grant toleration to protestant dissenters. And while many "court" Tories, in the aftermath of the exclusion crisis of 1679-81, were prepared to support a strong monarchy to prevent another period of instability and civil war, they drew back when James II's actions suggested he was contemplating the complete subjugation of Parliament and was heading towards a restructuring of the state along the lines of Louis XIV's France. The need to defend the Anglican church and Parliament prevented "court" supporters in England from endorsing the extreme statist position. Few English "court" supporters were prepared to see Parliament disappear completely, and nearly all of them were convinced that it was of the utmost importance to strengthen the Church of England and prevent any restoration of Catholicism. Thus conditions and personalities (particularly that of James II) made the "court" ideology a complex one in late seventeenth-century England. Still, it is possible to distinguish a "court" position that was essentially statist in outlook. The English "court" supporters wished the king to carry on government, keep up the established church, and turn to Parliament only when the need arose. The last four years of Charles II's reign showed the strength of these "court" sentiments. The king had abandoned his early toleration policies; he kept his Catholicism in check, and so he was able to exercise power from 1681 to 1685 without calling any Parliaments.[5]

The "country" spokesmen were suspicious of central power and looked to Parliament as an important check on aggrandisement of royal administration.

They were troubled by the absence of a dividing line between "court" values and Louis XIV's system. They feared kings might use a standing army and royal officials to increase government's reach into society by intervening in local government. They believed that monarchs, by use of bribery, patronage, and influence, tended to undermine the independence of Parliament and so create conditions in which the executive power, exercised through the Crown's ministers, became corrupt and tyrannical. "Country" attitudes tended to be more locally oriented, concerned with protecting traditional liberties and property rights against the encroaching power of royal government. While most "country" supporters set great store in the stabilizing influence of the Anglican church, the "country" leaders were prepared to enlist non-Anglican dissenters in the struggle against the creeping return of Catholicism under James II. In England, after 1679, the "country" objective was to prevent the English monarchy from developing along the lines of Louis XIV's France with its royal bureaucracy, its standing army, and its authority unchecked by a Parliament.[6]

The original Whig and Tory parties that coalesced during the exclusion crisis of 1679-81 and the ensuing ten years reflected these differing attitudes towards power and government. The Whigs claimed that James II planned to make all officials, local or national, dependent on the Crown alone, to undermine Parliament, and so to destroy Englishmen's properties and liberties. Appointment of Catholics at court and in the army and universities was taken as evidence of James's intentions. The Tories, who supported Charles II and James II up to 1688, believed it was dangerous to tamper with hereditary monarchy (as the Whigs had attempted to do in their efforts to exclude James from the succession) and that it was essential to rally round the court to prevent another period of political instability and perhaps even another civil war. In the English setting, the mainstream "court" position was tempered by two caveats. The Anglican church must be solidly maintained by the Crown and the independence of Parliament must be secure. It was James II's attack on church and Parliament that finally drove the Tories into opposition.[7]

With the flight of James II to France, it seemed that the "country" concept of central power would triumph in England, but this was not to be. The pre-1688 distinctions between "court" and "country" were subject to great pressure in the years between 1689 and 1720.[8] By the latter date, a fundamental realignment had taken place. The new regime faced years of expensive warfare against France, partly to help the Dutch interests of William but also to defend the revolutionary settlement against a French-backed restoration of James II and, after 1701, his son. The war effort required energetic and innovative stratagems by the ministers of William and Mary and Anne. Revenue had to be raised, loans managed, government credit established.

An army had to be kept in being from year to year; a navy had to be built up and maintained. In response to these pressures, Parliament began meeting every year to vote regular taxes, on the basis of which the government turned to the Bank of England to raise loans. A new, elaborate fiscal structure came into being with its twin features of a permanent national debt and a regular recourse by ministers to parliamentary taxation. By the late 1690's, many Tories saw the war as a Whig one that was bringing in its train many of the features of government which pre-1688 critics of the "court" position had claimed to fear.[9]

Within the Whigs themselves, there was growing tension between "old" Whigs who cleaved to the traditional "country" doctrine of small government and the "court" Whigs who, now that they had access to power, willingly embraced the financial revolution and the growth of administration weight and influence in the country and in Parliament. What had been an apparent victory for the "country" over the "court" in 1688-89 was transformed, much to the disgruntlement of Tories and old Whigs, into a new and flourishing version of "court"-style rule. The Whigs now supported the monarchy in a wholehearted manner; they accepted the national debt and all the associated system of taxation and fiscal management by the Crown's ministers and officials. The Bank of England was regarded as a Whig institution. They had established and kept in being a regular army; they had raised revenues to create the world's most powerful navy. To maintain their position, Whig ministers and magnates used crown patronage and other forms of influence in efforts to control Parliament. They even extended the life of Parliament (in the wake of the 1715 Jacobite scare) from three to seven years to make the task of parliamentary management easier, thus striking down the Triennial Act, one of the great "country" checks on central power passed by both Whigs and Tories in 1694. By 1720, the Whigs *were* the "court" party. The old Whig country opposition kept up a running attack on these developments, based on seventeenth-century "country" shibboleths. Critics of the system, like John Trenchard and Robert Gordon, made an impact on readers in the American colonies, but they made little impression on the political world of Walpolian England.[10]

As well as embracing these "court" concepts and practices, the great Whig politicians were part of a much narrower and more aristocratic ruling class than one might have expected to emerge after 1688. Between 1688 and 1714, elections were frequent and bitterly contested as the Triennial Act and deep Whig-Tory differences kept the political heat high. Elections became much more expensive to organize. Combined with the taxation arising from the French wars, the costliness of elections drove many of the lesser nobility and gentry out of active politics. By the 1720's, English national politics had become the preserve of an aristocratic oligarchy who monopolized the great

offices of central government and, through patronage and influence, manipulated the electoral system. As J.H. Plumb has shown, it was the ability of this
oligarchy to control Parliament effectively and (in co-operation with the new
Hanoverian kings) to control government that finally brought political stability to England, ending the major constitutional and religious disturbances of
the seventeenth century.[11] The forced abdication of James II in 1688 had not
produced stability. Instead, it had led to a twenty year period of bitter
partisan struggles between Whig and Tory over the nature of the constitution in church and state and over the need for, and consequences of, the
French wars. The Tory gentry might grumble at Whig hypocrisy and expediency;
the remnants of the old Whigs might have misgivings about the growth of
executive power; they both might be encouraged by the writings of Gordon
and Trenchard with their traditional radical critique of the new threats to
liberty; and some of the more cultivated might enjoy John Gay's satire of the
new corruption in *The Beggar's Opera* (1727), but all these opposition strains
had minimal impact on the dominance of "court" whiggery. The 1688-89
revolutionary settlement had run its course and ended up, through the
vagaries of circumstances and personality, by creating a centralized system
of "court" politics and finance.[12]

This orientation of the English political system remained in place for the
next fifty years until, in the 1760's, political parties began to develop in the
House of Commons and provide a new basis for ministerial stability. Throughout the eighteenth century, the Crown's ministers kept themselves in power
by influencing and managing the House of Commons. Royal sanction was
necessary to achieve office; parliamentary support was necessary to hold it.
This influencing of Parliament (especially the Commons) was regarded as a
natural and essential part of the balanced constitution. As David Hume
explained in 1741, "the crown has so many offices at its disposal that when
assisted by the honest and disinterested part of the house, it will always
command the resolution of the whole, so far, at least, as to preserve the
ancient constitution from danger. We may, therefore, give to this influence
what name we please, we may call it by the invidious appellations of
corruption and dependence; but some degree and some kind of it are
inseparable from the very nature of the constitution, and necessary to the
preservation of our mixed government."[13] Criticism of and opposition to the
system were always present, but as Lewis Namier has shown, up to the middle
decades of the eighteenth century, this opposition was no longer of the
coherent "country" variety, seeking to reduce influence in its myriad forms;
rather, it consisted of coalitions based on factional, family and personal
considerations.[14]

The pattern of "court" politics was strengthened in the last two decades of
the eighteenth century as the Tories, during the long reign of George III,

finally reverted to their natural position as supporters of the monarchy and as the French Revolution and the wars with France intensified attachment to British constitutional customs and the Hanoverian monarchy. As the American and French revolutions threatened with their more democratic concepts of government and as society in Britain became unsettled by the double impact of industrialization and war, a resurgent toryism formed around the "friends of Mr. Pitt," a process which led into the long period of Tory power under Lord Liverpool between 1812 and 1827.[15] Thus, during the eighteenth century and the early part of the nineteenth, both the Whig and Tory mainstreams , while they had developed renewed ideological differences in the 1760's, had left the classic "country" ideology far behind and had come to accept as normal an influential, central administration run by a landed ruling class responsive to a limited property-holding electorate. The aristocratic hold on power actually strengthened during the first two decades of the nineteenth century. "The upper classes," concluded A.D. Harvey in his meticulous account of this period, "were right up to the very eve of the 1832 Reform Act in the process of actually increasing their hold on the institutions in British society—the boroughs, the Church, the county administrations. The century which ended in the near eclipse of the aristocracy began with three decades during which they were at the height of their political and economic power."[16]

The 1688 revolution and its aftermath may have prevented an approximation to absolute monarchy from emerging in Britain, but the British monarchy was simply shifted along the spectrum to a point where it was made amenable to the interests and needs of the aristocracy and landed classes of the realm, stopping far short of the "country" concept of weak central government that had been so attractive in seventeenth-century England. The monarchy may have been limited after 1688, but government was not. It is true that throughout the eighteenth century, and as a reaction against James II's interventionism, local government in the counties remained the preserve of the country gentry, but central government and, perhaps more important, belief in the legitimacy of strong national regime were embedded in British political culture. As the prerogative powers of the monarchy waned, there emerged in Britain a national ruling class based largely on the landed aristocracy that occupied most high offices and oversaw the growth of his majesty's army, navy and bureaucracy. Between the 1760's and the 1820's, Whigs and Tories differed on the extent, nature and timing of central government intervention in society and the economy. The resources of British central government were admittedly weak compared to the administrative and police powers of some continental regimes and compared to the reach and resources of Victorian governments. But there was no longer any "country" challenge aimed at radically limiting the weight of British central

government, which, by the 1830's, was to undertake a series of national responses to the social and economic problems thrown up by industrialization.[17]

In the United States, the situation by the 1820's was the reverse of that in
Britain. In America, "country" triumphed over "court."[18] Such a departure
from the British path was not a foregone conclusion, although the geographical extent and diversity of the colonies, the absence of a dominant hereditary
landed class, the presence of a much larger proportion of property and
franchise holders, and the failure of an established church to extend its
binding tentacles, all conspired to make it difficult for "court"-type politics
to take root in eighteenth-century America. A fundamental difficulty in this
respect was the weakness of the royal governors. On paper, they had a great
deal of authority, in some ways more than the Crown itself in England. But
whereas the Crown and its ministers in England were able to deploy a wide
range of patronage and influence to manage Parliament and so enable the
government to carry on an effective administration, the colonial governors
found their positions very limiting. They did not have enough funds free of
assembly control, they did not have enough patronage, and they did not have
sufficient backing from enough locally influential social groups to enable
them to protect and exercise the power they had on paper. Most governors
found themselves on the defensive as assemblies throughout the period from
the 1690's to 1760's manoeuvred to define and circumscribe the limits to the
power of London-appointed governors.[19]

In spite of these formidable obstacles, several characteristics of "court"
regimes did begin to show signs of taking root in some northern colonies. In
Massachusetts, for example, under the administrations of William Shirley,
Thomas Pownall, and Thomas Hutchinson (1741-74), the royal governors
attempted, with some success, to use patronage and influence to build up a
class of officeholders and Anglicans who would constitute a naturally superior ruling group and act as a counterweight to the leveling tendencies in
colonial society. Governor Thomas Hutchinson (1770-74), especially, was
thoroughly attuned to the ways of establishment "court" whiggism of the
mid-eighteenth century. He believed the ability of the executive to act on
and influence society was healthy, natural, and necessary to maintain political and social stability. "For Hutchinson," explains Bernard Bailyn in his
authoritative biography, "as for Ramsay and the ruling Whig governments in
England the ultimate fact of political life . . . was the logical necessity for
an absolute and unitary authority to exist somewhere in every government;
in its essential definition that is what government was: a unit of absolute and
indivisible authority."[20] The existence of an assembly in the colonies or a
House of Commons in England ensured some scrutiny of government, but
the ability of the executive to manage assembly or commons was essential if
the administration was to exercise the necessary unitary power.

This insistence on the legitimacy of executive power and influence was easily incorporated into standard justifications of the British balanced or mixed constitution. In this context, Hutchinson shared with British "court" theorists, as they justified establishment whiggism, the conventional view that an assembly or commons that could not be influenced would lead to the usurpation of power by the democracy and the destruction of the balanced constitution. The cardinal point was that an independent commons had no place in the eighteenth-century British constitution. As William Blackstone explained in his *Commentaries on the Laws of England*, "a total disjunction" of Crown and Parliament "would be productive of tyranny" for the "legislative would soon become tyrannical by making continual encroachments and gradually assuming to itself the rights of executive power."[21] Acting with such basic assumptions in his mind, Hutchinson was deeply convinced that it was his right, indeed his duty, to use his appointive powers and his gubernatorial influence in an effort to bind together a class of local notables. He believed he should manage the local Massachusetts constitution in a similar manner as the "court" Whigs did in England.

Hutchinson's mistake, shared by all the colonial Tories and Loyalists, was to view colonial society as an extension of English society, developing towards English norms from rude beginnings in the seventeenth century. He thought as a provincial rather than a colonial settler or planter. This being so, he sought, as governor, to encourage the growth of those social and religious distinctions which marked out the ruling class of eighteenth-century England. It was this drift towards an Anglican upper class knit together by patronage that distressed educated, propertied and influential men, like John Adams, who fell outside the limits of Hutchinson's privileged circle.[22] There were too many in the colonies like Adams for the exclusive Hutchinson system to work. Such men deeply resented Hutchinson's blindness to the differences between English and colonial society, differences round which the newly conscious colonial patriotism began to form by the 1760's. The opposition began to articulate a "country" critique of the Hutchinson regime as a local system of influence and patronage that would lead to the imposition of an exclusive, corrupt, and all-powerful executive in the colony. This fitted easily into the general colonial critique of British policies after 1763, policies which seemed designed to buttress "court" tendencies in the colonies, policies which emanated from an English Parliament that, in the patriot view, had long lost its necessary independence.

If "court" tendencies showed patchy signs of success in northern colonies, in all the southern colonies the local constitutions worked in a typical "country" fashion. The houses of assembly in the southern royal colonies mounted a persistent series of stratagems from the late seventeenth century onwards that effectively clipped the wings of the governors and limited the influence of executive power within and out of doors.[23] The economic, social, and cultural conditions in the southern colonies led to this emasculation of central authority. There were no towns in the south comparable to Philadelphia or New York or Boston, functioning as economic and social magnets for increasingly integrated hinterlands. Economic centres were more localized and scattered. Perhaps most important of all was the nature of the planter class in the south. Dispersed over the countryside, enjoying local status and prestige, they were not a suitable base upon which governors might hope to build a clientele dedicated to the strengthening of central authority. Like the parliamentary gentry of pre-1640 England, these local notables in the southern colonies wanted small government, low taxes, and as much freedom as possible to organize their estates and their labour. They wanted to be left alone to grow and sell their crops. It was no accident that during the revolutionary era, it was this southern planter class that produced the most eloquent and informed spokesmen of the "country" ideology. Set on their local estates, with their poor controlled as slaves, the Virginia planters like Jefferson were one group in the Anglo-American world of the mid-eighteenth century which could embrace unreservedly the "country" ideology as the best guide to organizing government and society.[24]

Under the pressure of the 1763-74 attempts by Britain to make imperial and parliamentary policies more effective in the colonies, the American patriot ideology came to rely heavily on this traditional "country" critique of corrupt and over-powerful central authority threatening long-cherished local liberties. The beefing up of the customs service, the changes in policy with respect to judges' pay and appointments, the use of admiralty courts, the quartering of troops, the attempts to raise more revenue were all taken by the patriots as evidence that George III's ministers were seeking to duplicate in the colonies conditions that already enabled them to suborn Parliament in England. The new posts available and the new monies raised by the parliamentary measures of the 1760's would finally permit the British governors to pay less heed to the assemblies, to expand the appointive world of executive government, and so to fasten onto the colonies' governor-controlled administrations impervious to the wishes of the people. In making their critique of British policies, the patriots drew extensively on the writings of those radical commonwealthmen like James Harrington and Algernon Sydney who had attacked similar developments in England during the seventeenth century and on early eighteenth-century critics like Trenchard and Gordon who had inherited this radical tradition.[25] But whereas in Britain, the old "country" rhetoric appealed only to a small minority by the 1720's, in the American colonies a much larger number of propertied, educated, and franchise-wielding individuals saw the dangers of having an unchecked executive placed over them. In England after 1688, the "country" ideology had been shunted off down a side-road; in America, colonial conditions made it popular.

The revolutionary experience altered this "country" ideology into American republican forms as the new states attempted to solve the constitutional problems by doing away with monarchy altogether, by defining separate executive and legislative spheres and by making government, whenever possible, a task to be undertaken by elected rather than appointed officials.[26] The new republican ideology seemed to be generally accepted in the 1780's, but as the new nation experienced fiscal and economic difficulties, the concept of strong central government took a new lease on life and had one last fling in the 1790's before the long nineteenth-century run of weak national governments. To Alexander Hamilton and like-minded Federalists, independence could only be successful if the United States followed the course which had brought Britain to world economic leadership. The new nation, reasoned the Federalists, required a central government that could maintain domestic law and order, deal effectively in international diplomacy, stabilize the economy by establishing a central bank to duplicate the function of the Bank of England, and defend American territory and protect American shipping on the high seas. Although some critics charged Hamilton with secret plans to re-establish the monarchy and all its associated corrupting influences, there is no evidence that he wished to turn the clock back. He was attempting, within the new republican setting, to map out a course that would bring the United States down the already successful English path to political stability and economic prosperity.

The Federalists' greatest strength throughout the 1790-1815 years lay in the New England states where, in the colonial period, some approximation to "court" political cultures had flickered fitfully into life, but the anglophilia of the Federalists, their penchant for hierarchy, and their hankering after deference convinced too many democratic Americans that revolutionary and republican achievements were being threatened by the reintroduction of a British-style, quasi-monarchical form of national government. The Democratic-Republican opposition, solidly strong in the southern states where economic growth was not seen to require elaborate initiatives by central government, redoubled their efforts under Jefferson and his Virginian successors to preserve the virtuous republic which had been created by freeing America from corrupt Britain. These Democratic-Republicans won in 1800 and so thwarted Federalist hopes of building up a more directive national government. After 1800, the Federalists declined as a political force, unable to impose their more traditional view of government and society on the geographically immense, ethnically varied landscape of democratic and republican America.[27]

By this time, English envoys in Washington and British governors in

Canada had a lively awareness of the weakness of the national government in the United States. They were contemptuous of its ability to influence the destabilizing cross-currents of politics or even to control its anarchic citizenry.[28] The consequence of revolution was a small and weak central government. Without a national governing class, without (as yet) an integrated national economy, with deep sectional differences, with its characteristic localism and with its revolutionary myths to cherish, America was fertile ground for the apotheosis of the "country" view of government. As Eric Foner has pointed out, it took the civil war to make a nation of the United States.[29] By the 1820's, the "court" had won in Britain, but in America the "country" controlled completely the field of political battle.[30]

The differing social, economic, and political conditions in Britain and her American colonies had led to a fundamental divergence in their politico-constitutional courses. Conditions were different yet again in Britain's colony of Canada; as a result, that colony charted out a third and peculiar mutation of British constitutional and political forms. Canada, it is conventionally thought, falls somewhere between the American and British political systems, but taking stock of the situation in the 1820's, Canada's local constitution was, in fact, even more "court" in its assumptions and operation than that of Britain itself.

From the outset, the type of constitution in Canada was affected by two factors that made Canada significantly different from the other British colonies in North America. First, Canada was acquired through military conquest and diplomatic bargaining which ended with the Peace of Paris in 1763. As Benjamin Franklin and other patriot leaders well understood as they made their critique of Britain, the fact that the American colonies had not been conquered by British arms before settlement but had originated as settler communities with charter privileges was of the highest significance. This was the crucial starting point for arguing that certain colonial-settler rights stemming from seventeenth-century charters could not be invaded by a later British government. A little-known but revealing example of this mode of thinking is the colony of Nova Scotia, which did not join the rebellion in 1776. Nova Scotia had been settled by New Englanders in the 1760's, but these people knew they had moved to land won by British arms. They had settled on conquered territory, and they were unsure if any of their traditional New England liberties remained.[31]

Second, Canada's population, following the British conquest was, apart from British officials, army men and merchants, entirely a French-speaking community, completely oblivious to all the "court" and "country" shibboleths that had preoccupied the Anglo-American political world of the seventeenth and eighteenth centuries. These two factors, combined with British misgivings about developments in the Ohio country and the thirteen coastal colonies, led to the decision not to establish any elected institutions at all in the colony. Even after the return to peacetime rule in 1764, the governors remained officers in the British army. All executive power lay securely with the governor and his appointed council. The Quebec Revenue Act of 1774, as noted, sanctioned the collection of revenues by this unchecked executive.[32] For the next twenty-seven years, until the constitutional changes of 1791, Canada had the most extreme form of "court" constitution ever seen in Britain or her other North American colonies.

The new French-speaking population accepted this system with equanimity—on the surface.[33] It provided stability and security to life and property which came as a relief after long years of debilitating warfare that had brought famine to the streets of Montreal. Moreover, as objects of conquest, the French Canadians might have expected harsher treatment. After all, their fellow colonists and co-religionists in Nova Scotia, the Acadians, had been physically removed from their ancestral lands by the British as recently as 1755-58. Their acceptance of the new British regime was encouraged by the single most influential institution, the Catholic church, whose very existence now came to depend on its accommodating relationship with the British authorities. From the mid-1760's onwards, the Quebec church, permitted by the Crown to collect tithes, train priests, and maintain its parish organizations, became a dedicated defender of the new administration. The mass of the habitants did not become British patriots, but they did come to accept the British constitutional order under which they now lived. They were at peace and freed from militia duty, and they even began to experience some economic prosperity as the West Indian and British markets opened up for Canadian lumber and agricultural products. On top of these expedient reasons, the French-speaking population found nothing philosophically odd about the British regime. The habitants had always lived under an authoritarian monarchy; they accepted that as the natural state form. They expected government to come from above, by way of appointed officialdom, without any mediating force of representative institutions. They were used to hierarchy in society and government. These traditional values of the French Canadians predisposed them to accept the "court" style constitution. Their acceptance was all the more willing since the British took pains to adjust government as far as possible to meet the needs of his majesty's new subjects. The Quebec Act of 1774, with its formal recognition of existing law and custom, was confirmation of the basic benevolence of the post-conquest regime. Insofar as there was an opposition, it came in English voices from merchants who worked to have a colonial assembly as part of their efforts to anglicize the legal and business environment in the St. Lawrence Valley.[34]

If the fact of military conquest and the nature of the French-Canadian predicament determined the initial shape of British constitutional forms in

Canada, the first major alteration of these forms was caused by the influx of thousands of Loyalists who settled in pockets along the north shore of the St. Lawrence and Lake Ontario. It was the Loyalist presence, more than any other factor, that finally convinced the Pitt government that representative institutions would have to be established in Canada. The Loyalist migration and later additions created an English settler society beyond Montreal. As long as the Canadian population was mainly French, the British had been able to temporize on matters of constitutional liberty. But now that an English population was in place, it was necessary to concede that mixed or balanced constitution with its representative component that eighteenth-century Englishmen believed to be a birthright both in the mother country and the colonies. But the constitution that was finally worked out for Upper and Lower Canada in 1791 was a strange creation, significantly affected as it was by loyalist ideology and the growing toryism of Pitt's administration in London. The Canadas, in fact, never received their local version of the much vaunted mixed constitution.

Loyalists' concepts of government and society were an unusual mixture, based on British and colonial practices but affected by their experiences at the hands of American republicans during the war years. As a guiding credo, the Loyalists believed that the American patriots were extremists, intent on leveling the familiar contours of the anglo-colonial landscape. As we have seen in the case of Thomas Hutchinson, Loyalists thought an effective, unitary executive power with legitimate means of influencing the assemblies was essential for political and social stability. Loyalists were convinced that deference was an additional, essential characteristic of the good society.[35] In this sense, they were practical believers in the benefits brought by the classical concept of deference that J.G.A. Pocock has described as the basis of much conventional eighteenth-century political thought.[36] The Loyalists assumed there was a natural hierarchy in society and that propertied and churched men were to constitute the political nation. In so thinking, they reasoned that in the English and colonial settings, where governments did not possess the policing powers of absolute monarchies, deferential acceptance of place was the key to preserving constitutional liberty. Without deference, governments would either resort to tyranny or be taken over by the democracy. Once that key of deference was thrown away, as the patriots thoughtlessly failed to see, the door was open to a novel concept that would usher in an unstable, property-threatening democracy. As well as being intimately tied to their views on deference, the Loyalists were absolutely attached to monarchy with all its associated techniques of appointive rather than elective administration. In the increasingly open and competitive colonial societies of the 1760's and early 1770's, the Loyalists rightly regarded monarchy as the institutional and psychological means of guaranteeing hierarchy and deference.[37]

Deference, hierarchy, and monarchy were their watchwords, but the Loyalists were also creatures of the eighteenth-century British world and thus uncomfortable with a constitutional system lacking any representative branch, the strange condition they found when they settled in Canada. For their part, the British government, while they had been willing to take advantage of the peculiar French-Canadian presence to avoid or delay the granting of an assembly, well understood that with thousands of English settlers (and with hopes of more to come), some version of the mixed eighteenth century constitution, including an elected house, would now have to be implemented in Canada. As they approached this matter, Pitt's ministers and advisers bore in mind two lessons. Signs that the French Revolution was not going to be as respectable as England's "bloodless revolution" of 1688 and the beginnings of serious unrest connected with industrialization in England confirmed their fears of mob influence. And as they remembered their experiences in the thirteen now independent colonies, they recalled how the lower houses there had managed to gain so much ascendancy over the governors and executive councils. It was determined that the constitution of the Canadas would exclude the possibility of too much democracy and would be so constructed as to avoid a repetition of the American pattern.

With these factors at work, it is not surprising that the 1791 constitution, while conceding representative assemblies in Upper and Lower Canada, deliberately created an exceptionally strong "court" orientation. British ministers hoped to establish a political and constitutional system in the Canadas that would make British forms and practices resistant to the corrosive levelling tendencies of North America. With this consideration in mind, they shielded the governor and his appointed executive council from potential democratic undermining. All executive power remained with a powerful governor and his council. All administrative appointments, the entire patronage in each colony, lay at the disposal of the governor and the officials on his council. Moreover, the terms of the Quebec Revenue Act continued in force, which meant that the executive was able to collect and appropriate substantial crown revenues such as customs without reference to the assemblies.[38]

A telling sign of the determination to prevent the 1791 constitution going down the same path as those of the Thirteen Colonies was the role and composition of the legislative councils. The legislative councils were to be nominated by the Crown, and it was hoped that they would become as weighty and influential as the House of Lords in the British setting. The councils were designed to coax into existence a class of hereditary aristocrats, locally equivalent to the British peerage. The prospective lieutenant-governor of Upper Canada, James Simcoe, expected he would have "a hereditary council with some mark of nobility," and he was given just that. The 1791 act (31 George III, c. 31) provided specifically for this, stipulating in section VI that the Crown could create Canadian peers who would have "a hereditary right of being summoned to the Legislative council." The "general object," Lord Grenville explained, was that "this Plan is to assimilate the constitution of that Province to that of Great Britain as nearly as the differences arising from the manners of the People and from the present situation of the Province will admit."[39]

Besides a hereditary upper house, the 1791 act also attempted to ensure that the Anglican church would function as the established church in Upper Canada. Articles on the church issue referred to the need to maintain "a protestant clergy" and provided for public lands to be set aside in each township for parsonages or rectories "according to the establishment of the Church of England." As he contemplated such developments, Simcoe congratulated himself on having an Anglican establishment to buttress his power and assure stability. "I am to have a Bishop," he wrote, and then explained how such an established church would mould the development of the colony. "The state propriety of some form of public worship practically considered, arises from the necessity there is of preventing the enthusiastic and fanatic teachers from acquiring that superstitious hold of the multitude."[40]

The proposed hereditary upper chamber and state church were measures designed to ensure that the governor and his executive, backed by the hereditary legislative council and the preaching of an established clergy, would be able to keep the multitude out of government and under control. An elected assembly was granted because a representative house was a necessary part of the post-1688 mixed constitution. It would ensure that people of property would be permanently represented; it would act as a sounding board for governor and his councils; and it would give advice and play its necessary role in drafting new legislation. But the assemblies were not to have prime responsibility for raising or appropriating revenue. The assembly was not intended to become the initiating element in the constitution. The centre of gravity was to lie in the "court" with the governor surrounded by his appointed executive council, the hereditary upper house, and a church establishment.

Such were the British plans and hopes in 1791, to organize a constitution that, in spite of unfavourable North American conditions, would work like the British constitution, complete with a local House of Lords. It is revealing that within the colony of Upper Canada, the new constitution was criticized by some leading Loyalists from the vantage point of their American background. Richard Cartwright, for example, complained that too many officials in the legislative council would destroy its independence.[41] But those who implemented the new constitution, particularly Lieutenant-Governor Simcoe in

Upper Canada, were sure they were "establishing a free honourable British Government, and a pure administration of its laws which shall hold out to the solitary immigrants, and to the several states, advantages that under the present form of government they do not and cannot enjoy."[42] The Canadas were to prove that monarchy, hierarchy, and deference would lead to stability and good government. They were to be an exemplary counterpoint to the United States with its weak government and its chaotic democracy.

But British vision was blinkered in 1791, as it had been on American colonial matters throughout the eighteenth century. The big problem in arranging colonial constitutions after 1688 was that a huge discrepancy existed between the way the British constitution actually worked and the way in which British ministers believed it ought to work in the colonies. In the old colonial system, and again with the Canadian constitution of 1791, there was no provision for any co-operation between assembly and the executive. No provision was made because there was no such provision in the British constitution; yet, the British system only worked because the Crown was willing to choose many of its chief ministers from the Commons. Robert Walpole, Lord North, and William Pitt all remained in the Commons. Nothing was fixed about this, of course, and between 1812 and 1827, Liverpool was prime minister from the Lords, leaving Castlereagh to lead in the Commons. Still, any British cabinet did need to manage the Commons and seek its co-operation for public measures. All this, however, depended on custom and usage rather than any constitutional principle. The trick was how to transfer this custom and usage to the colonial settings.

The British formula never did take root in the American colonies. Colonial politics, as Bailyn and Greene have shown, was characterized by a confrontational relationship between governors, their councillors, and the assemblies. Instead of being brought together into a political relationship, colonial executives and assemblies operated from separate competitive spheres. Co-operation between executives and assemblies had been missing in the American colonies and in 1791, a system had again been established in the Canadas that made such a working relationship on British lines unlikely to emerge. Indeed, the situation was even more hopeless in the Canadas; the governor and his councillors controlled revenue and patronage to such an extent that there was no reason why they should seek to build up anything more than a minimal political relationship with the assemblies. "Government," wrote Governor General Dalhousie, "has the purse and Revenue in hand to pay its way." Consequently, "a successful attempt to make the executive submit to the legislature, though possible in Great Britain, was impossible in Canada."[43]

Simcoe believed a British constitution had been set up in 1791, but the Canada Act established a contentious constitutional structure. As Lord

Durham cogently put it when he reported on Canada in 1839: "the natural state of government in all these Colonies is that of collision between the executive and the representative body."[44] It was in this setting that Canadian attitudes towards government and politics began to take shape.

For the French Canadians in Lower Canada, representative institutions like the assembly were novel. Their responses to the new British regime became more complex than in the 1760–91 period when they had accepted the customary government from above. Because of their overwhelming demographic strength, French Canadians were able, from the outset, to dominate the assembly. This numerical superiority could not be brought to bear on government because the new constitution gave the assembly a relatively marginal role in raising and spending revenues. The situation became tense after about 1800, by which time social, economic, and educational conditions within Lower Canada produced sharp resentments which were voiced through the francophone majority in the assembly. A new social class was emerging and began to criticize the rigidities and biases of the 1791 constitution. Young men, educated at the collèges classiques for the liberal professions, were entering society in such numbers that they came directly up against the barriers protecting the exclusive governing and official class. Frustrated in their career ambitions and increasingly indignant that the representative system of 1791 was doing little to open doors to French Canadians, this class of new men turned to politics and mounted a campaign inside and outside the assembly against the Chateau Clique, which, from its base in the appointed executive and legislative councils, monopolized public offices.[45] Leaders of le parti canadien argued that although there were some French Canadians on the councils, this limited degree of collaboration obscured the fact that the French Canadian middle class was being altogether ignored in the business of running the country. From that starting point, the opposition leaders in the assembly were able to make a plausible nationalist case that the great mass of French Canadians were being imposed upon by a narrow, predominantly English ruling clique.[46]

The entire system in Lower Canada was maintained, entrenched, and strengthened by the range of patronage available to the governor and his councillors. They could make appointments and allocate salaries for every post from customs officer to judge in a conscious effort to create an anglicized ruling class—and under the terms of the 1791 constitution, they could do this without paying much heed to the assembly. This being the case, the conflict between executive and assembly revolved round the issue of patronage, its distribution was the grand technique for cementing the ruling political alliance.[47] Le parti canadien leaders in the assembly did not call for the scaling down of excessive government. Instead, they urged that the system be opened up so that more French Canadians could occupy positions of power and responsibility. They wished to gain access to the system and derive benefits from it.

Since the conflict took place within the anglicized institutional context created in 1791, a context in which "court" and "country" parties had competed in an effort to impose the preferred type of government, there were sparks of "country" rhetoric aimed at the Chateau Clique in Lower Canada. But it is revealing that no classic "country" opposition, dedicated to solving the patronage problem by reducing the size of government, took root in Lower Canada. As the local colonial elite and British Tory governments up to 1830 and even the post-1830 Whig administrations in London remained unbending, some opposition leaders were driven into more extreme denunciations. By the 1830's, Louis-Joseph Papineau, the Reform leader in Lower Canada, had something of the classic "country" ideologue about him. On his seigneural country estate north of Montreal with its local chapel and with his determination to manage his lands and woods efficiently, Papineau can almost be cast in a Jeffersonian mould as an enlightened country notable, determined to limit the size and impact of monarchical government.[48] This facet of Papineau was later caught in remarks made by Lady Monck as she drove past Papineau's estate at Montebello—Papineau in a gesture of aristocratic magnanimity had left some flowers for the Prince of Wales's party at the entrance to his estate.[49] Papineau's refusal to enter the administration of Governor Metcalfe in 1844 also fits this pattern of an aloof figure who worked to keep his distance from the corrupting world of power and patronage. But this rarefied image of Papineau caused some problems in 1837-38, and it was one of the reasons, after his return, that he remained an isolated, if worshipped, political figure.[50]

The mainstream of opposition in Lower Canada remained "court" and statist. It wanted to be taken aboard rather than to sink the government ship. They did not even wish to change the captain, for as the failure of the 1837 rising and events of the 1840's and 1850's were to demonstrate, the French Canadians were quite content to accept British monarchical government, providing they could fully participate in it.[51] This statist mentality had deep roots in the French colonial past and remained a profound influence throughout modern Quebec's political development, as has been amply demonstrated by the role of the "state middle classes" in Quebec of the 1970's and 1980's.[52] With these traditions and mentalities, the question of gaining access to government and office was critical in Lower Canada. It was necessary to break open that comprehensive system of patronage and share in it to the fullest extent justified by overwhelming demographic superiority. Thus, in Lower Canada, politics focused on the patronage question. On the one side, imperial officeholders and their local allies sought to control spending and engross patronage. On the other side, the opposition fought to seize these instruments of power from the anglicized elite and the remnants of the former seigneural elite. It was a struggle for local sovereignty. One side sought to maintain effective control of the colonial state; the opponents worked to displace them and take over the local state apparatus. Power meant patronage, and that was what both sides were interested in.[53]

If we turn to the English settlers in Upper Canada during this same period, from the 1790's to the 1820's, there was, although for a differing set of reasons, a similar acceptance of "court" values and a similar appreciation by the Reformers of the importance of patronage. In Upper Canada, the population was so small and so preoccupied with survival in the first two decades that the executive was as unchallenged as the constitution intended it to be (although there were individual critics). The military and diplomatic tensions with the United States and the increasing number of settlers coming in from the new republic led the local elite in Upper Canada to stick hard to the tenets of exclusivity, making it difficult for the assembly to have any impact on government. After 1815, as the local economy grew and as immigrants began to flow in from Britain, the number and social importance of those excluded increased to the point where systematic and organized opposition began to appear in the assembly.[54] As in Lower Canada, the contemptuous intransigence of the ruling alliance (styled the Family Compact by exasperated Reformers) led opposition leaders into extreme positions by the 1830's. In his final furious stage following his election defeat in 1836, William Lyon Mackenzie, the radical Reform leader, opted for independence, republicanism, and democracy (besides biblical egalitarianism).[55] But the mainstream reform movement, best characterized by the Baldwin family, remained committed to monarchy, hierarchy, and executive control of patronage. Robert Baldwin simply wanted to shift the entire system from a narrow to a broad base in the community. When Baldwin finally held power, he distributed patronage as freely as had the Family Compact. The *Colonial Gazette*, mouthpiece of the colonial reformers in England, complained that Baldwin, LaFontaine, and the Canadian Reformers (once they achieved power after 1848) were trying "by engrossing all the patronage to make themselves as powerful a family compact as that which they have trodden down." They were doing so to break down the old, exclusive system of Anglican, compact-tory officeholding. Baldwin was never interested in reducing or weakening government. Throughout his life he believed in strong, effective executive influence. As Lord Elgin perceptively remarked, Baldwin wished to bring about change without undermining the existing monarchical constitution.[56]

Taking stock of the Canadas by the 1820's makes clear the extent to which these two British North American colonies had diverged from both the British and American paths of development and were setting their own peculiar course. Using as reference points the polarities of "country" America and "court" England, the peculiarity lay in the fact that the Canadas were even more "court" in their working constitutions than Britain. The conquest origins, the traditional nature of French colonial society, and the needs of the British imperial government led to authoritarian government between 1764 and 1791, during which time the executive acted without any checks whatsoever from representative institutions. The impact of Loyalists' views on hierarchy, deference, and democracy and the growing anti-democratic fears in Pitt's government and in the minds of British governors from the 1790's to the 1820's ensured that when a representative branch was added, the constitution of the two colonies remained "court" in orientation. All power was located with the governor and his councillors, backed by legislative councils that were designed to become hereditary chambers and which were in fact controlled by officials, and by a government-sustained Anglican church in Upper Canada and a subservient Roman Catholic Church in Lower Canada.

Measured against contemporary British practices, the Canadas now had an excessively "court" system of government. In Britain, ever since the initial years between 1688 and 1714, when the demands of the French wars had led to annual sessions of Parliament and a working relationship between it and the Crown, Parliament had remained a permanent part of the working constitution. By the end of the eighteenth century, during the administrations of Pitt, the Commons was playing an even more active role in scrutinizing government expenditures and thus in influencing policy on the getting and spending of public money. The Crown and Lords were still of great importance as separate centres of political power, but by the 1820's no king or his ministers could govern without paying systematic attention to the Commons and managing regular majorities. In contrast, within Upper and Lower Canada after 1791, the governing classes proceeded on the basis that the assemblies had an absolutely subsidiary role, as providers of occasional advice, drafters of laws, and occasional suppliers of additional revenue; in the normal course of events, the assemblies should have no role in deciding either the composition of the administration or in formulating policy on public issues.

This "court" orientation became so deeply embedded in the Canadas that even the opposition accepted its assumptions. Given the contest between executive and assemblies, each in their separate spheres, it might have been expected that a Canadian variant of classic eighteenth-century "country" opposition would emerge, clamouring for a permanent reduction of these bloated and corrupt governments. But no such ideological attack was made. Radical proposals did surface later in the rebellion period from 1836 to 1838, but the mainstream of opposition from the 1790's to the 1840's never embraced the rhetoric that had appealed to so many in the American colonies. Historical conditions hardly left room for such rhetoric in the Canadas. Attachment to monarchy, to appointive officialdom, and to some degree of hierarchy were values shared by the Loyalists, French Canadians, and post-1815 British immigrants.

Moreover, the proximity of the democratic republic placed limits on Canadian oppositions. To push opposition too far could quickly be tainted with the brush of disloyalty. Moving too far towards some democratic check on the executive, a natural development even in Britain, was easily portrayed in the Canadas as an attempt to introduce American-style republicanism which would not simply reform government but would weaken it and make it the prey of organized special interests. An attack on the constitutional system which allowed crown-appointed governors and their councils so much power could be represented (as Lieutenant-Governor Head represented it in 1836 in Upper Canada) as an attack on monarchy and the British connection in favor of annexation and republicanism.[57] The proximity of the United States made "country" rhetoric a dangerous weapon for its wielders in Canada. It could lead readily to self-inflicted wounds. This was a phenomenon that Canadian opponents of government were to discover to their cost for the whole period down to 1911. Thus, because of internal conditions and the threatening proximity of the American democracy, the opposition leaders who carried respect, men like Baldwin and LaFontaine, did not talk in terms of dismantling the system, reducing government, or cutting into the range of executive influence and patronage. Rather, they talked in terms of opening up the system and making the executive more responsive to the assembly, as in Britain. They aimed at a much wider range of participation so that public policy would rest on a sounder base and so that more individuals and groups could share in the benefits of monarchical government. They did not wish to reduce executive power; they wished to take it over and exercise it.

This dialectic between government and opposition produced a characteristic feature of Canadian political culture that had an impact right down to 1914 and beyond. The ruling elites in the Canadas, composed of imperial officials and their local upper class collaborators, depended after 1791 on patronage deployment to maintain their privileged positions in a North American setting that was typically unfavourable for hierarchy, deference and state churches. The Family Compact and Chateau Clique consisted of networks of local notables tied together by patronage.[58] Opposition critics among the Reformers and *le parti canadien* who wished to remain loyal pointed to the unfair exclusivity of the system and the narrow social groups who benefited from it. They concentrated their efforts on breaking into these patronage networks as the principal technique of changing the character of government without making dangerous proposals for radical structural constitutional change. Patronage, to be sure, was a feature of early nineteenth-century politics both in Britain and the United States, but Canadian politics was much more explicitly *about* patronage.[59] Patronage had come to occupy the centre stage in Canadian politics.

2

INSTABILITY, 1828-1864

The twenty-five or so years from the late 1820's to the mid-1850's were the equivalent in Canada to the critical periods between 1689 and 1720 in England and 1763 to 1789 in the American colonies and the United States. In England, the 1688-89 revolution had left unsettled many basic questions about the constitution in church and state, and the years down to 1714 were characterized by bitter party battles as Whigs and Tories sought to impose their views about the place of the Anglican church, the relationship between Crown and Parliament, and whether or not the wars with France were in the national interest. In America, the attack on British policies and the colonial critique of the workings of the British constitution led to independence, the abandonment of monarchy, and the adoption of a new republican constitution to make radical changes in the now discredited British system. The course in the Canadas was not as dramatic as that in the American colonies and states, but this was still a decisive, formative period as ever more distinctive Canadian institutions, practices, and attitudes emerged from the ruins of the 1791 constitution.

Instability became the hallmark of Canadian politics from the late 1820's onwards. The year 1828 is a useful benchmark for the beginning of this period of deep uncertainty over the constitutional structure. In that year, a British parliamentary committee acknowledged the validity of some basic charges against the working of the 1791 constitution, and from that point on, particularly when the new Whig administrations came to power in England after 1830, the local ruling groups in the Canadas were never sure of the necessary support from Britain for the continuance of the 1791 constitutional structures.[1] The governing elites in Upper and Lower Canada, the

Family Compact and the Chateau Clique, struggled desperately to hold on to their exclusive system. They looked with increasing dismay to England as successive imperial administrations appeared to countenance their Reform opponents and accept the possibility of changes that would open up the system of government. The Howick Act passed in 1831 (1 and 2 William IV, c. 23), which provided for the assemblies to take a bigger role in the appropriation of the Crown's revenues, was an ominous portent from the viewpoint of the governing Tories.[2] The Reform movements in both Canadas took heart from these apparent shifts in British policy in the late 1820's and early 1830's and intensified their efforts to gain control of the assembly in Upper Canada and, in both Canadas, to use the weight of the popular assemblies to break down the barriers of privilege protecting the ruling politicians and officials with their myriad of connections.

Elections became more frequent, as they had been in England between 1688 and 1714 when fundamental questions about the constitution and power were at stake. In Upper Canada, elections took place in 1828, 1830, 1834, and 1836, and in the Union of the Canadas in 1841, 1844 and 1848, seven elections within twenty years, each of them bitterly contested. At every one of these elections, contemporaries believed basic questions about the constitution and the very nature of politics were at stake. In Lower Canada, there was no series of elections through the 1830's, but the situation was even more tense and confrontational because the French-Canadian Reformers could control the assembly much more easily than their counterparts in Upper Canada. There was a direct constitutional standoff between the assembly and the governor and council as the assembly used the new possibilities of the Howick Act to attempt to stop supplies. In 1838, the constitution of Lower Canada was suspended altogether, and the colony was run by a specially appointed council until representative government was restored in the Union. Throughout the 1830's, governors and lieutenant-governors were convinced they were fighting a decisive battle against American-style republicanism and democracy, the triumph of which would lead to the end of monarchy and the loss of the colonies. The "fate of the Canadas" was at stake.[3]

The political turbulence broke out into open rebellion in 1837 as frustrated Reform leaders despaired of changes coming through a system controlled and manipulated by the governors and their Tory allies. These rebellions further deepened the bitter partisanship; Tories labelled all Reformers as pro-American traitors and blamed the imperial authorities for countenancing their grievances. By the late 1830's, Tories were "incensed beyond all expression" at the course of events in Upper Canada.[4]

To all these signs of the troubled times, two more complicating dimensions were added by the creation of the Union of the Canadas in 1840-41. In the former Lower Canada, the Reform supporters of Louis Hippolyte LaFontaine now tried to stick together, win enough seats in the assembly, and use this political strength to protect their language and culture from the assimilative intent of the Union. They were in a struggle to protect their nationality. Also at stake, after 1840, was the nature of the constitution. All but the diehard Tories knew that the old, exclusive system could not continue without major alterations, but there was wide and sharp disagreement about the timing and content of these alterations. From the unreconstructed Tory view at one end of the spectrum of possibilities (that the governor should rely only on the loyal "constitutional party") to the Reform view (that political leaders with a majority in the assembly should head the council), there was a range of options about the precise degree of prerogative power the governor should retain. These deep uncertainties meant that there was no relief from the political turmoil of the 1830's.

Indeed, politics became even more heated as French Canadians fought for lost rights, and Reformers, moderate Conservatives, and Tories fought over the relationship between Crown and Parliament or, in Canadian terms, between governor and assembly. In 1845, that old Anglican Tory, John Strachan, lamented that ever since the Union had been established, "all is political agitation."[5] Four governors within the space of five years between 1840 and 1845 only increased the sense of uncertainty and political flux. In these circumstances, Canadian political groupings of Reformers and Tories fought as they had never fought before to win seats in the assembly and so be in a position to enforce their view of how the constitution should operate. The Tory outrage over the Rebellion Losses Bill in 1849 and the burning of the parliament building in Montreal were the culminating symbolic events of these troubled years and dramatic signs of how deep feelings ran. "Never had party ferocity reached such a pitch in Canada," wrote J.C. Dent in his contemporary account of these years.[6] This was, indeed, a "most eventful period." As Etienne Parent summed it up, this had been "une époque mémorable de notre histoire."[7]

It was a turbulent period because the 1791 constitution worked so badly. It failed miserably because there developed a huge discrepancy between actual conditions in the Canadas and the theoretical and practical considerations upon which the constitution was based. The 1791 Canada Act was supposed to give the Canadas a constitution that would work like the British one. But the framers of the constitution and the British imperial officials who operated it in North America failed to appreciate the significance of the central element of the eighteenth-century British constitution. The system was successful because there was a working relationship between the Crown's ministers and Parliament. Nothing in the 1688-89 settlement laid down any rules for establishing such a relationship and British constitutional law was not forthcoming on the issue, but this political co-operation was essential for the effective functioning of the British constitution.

Earl Grey, the British Whig statesman in the 1820's, 1830's, 1840's who prided himself on his knowledge of such great matters, explained in his *Parliamentary Government* how necessary it was to comprehend the difference between theoretical definitions of the British balanced constitution and how it actually worked. "Since the establishment of Parliamentary Government, the common description of the British constitution as one in which the executive power belongs exclusively to the Crown while the power of legislation is vested jointly in the Sovereign and the two Houses of Parliament, has ceased to be correct, unless it is understood as applying only to the legal and technical distribution of power. It is the distinguishing characteristic of Parliamentary government that it requires the powers belonging to the Crown to be exercised through Ministers who are held responsible for the manner in which they are used, who are expected to be members of the two Houses of Parliament, the proceedings of which they must be able generally to guide and who are considered entitled to hold their offices only while they possess the confidence of Parliament and more especially the House of Commons."[8] There was then a disjunction between the theoretical basis of the British constitution and the way it worked in practice. This disjunction was not taken into account by the framers of the 1791 constitution or by the British governors who operated it from the 1790's to the 1830's.

Whereas in Britain administration depended on a working harmony between ministers of the Crown and Parliament, there was no equivalent intermingling of executive council and assembly in the Canadas. Governors and their executive councillors could make serious and prolonged efforts to function independently of assembly wishes. The executive councillors were chosen by the governor in consultation with the imperial government. Down to the 1830's, most members of the executive councils in both Upper and Lower Canada, whether British- or Canadian-born, regarded their appointments as individual patent offices to be held for life. These men were not the equivalent of British cabinet members; they were permanent crown officials, "gens de place" as they were called in Lower Canada.[9] Even the legislative councils had a preponderance of officials who had no need to respond to political pressure from the assembly or from the country. The legislative councils were rightly regarded as bastions of official and gubernatorial power rather than as chambers representing any section of the community. So entrenched were many high officials of the executive council that even the governor had difficulties supervising and controlling their department work. The governor and his executive councillors had untrammelled control of crown revenues and crown patronage and used their appointive powers to build up exclusive ruling connections in both Canadas without establishing a British-type relationship with the assemblies.

As long as the population was small in Upper Canada, the system did work, but as population built up and the economy developed after 1815, many new groups, interests, and individuals suffered from the exclusive system. Criticism in the assembly became more coherent and organized. In Lower Canada, as we have seen, because of the contrast between a largely francophone assembly and a largely anglophone executive and official class, the confrontation emerged earlier and more sharply, particularly as new members of the French Canadian professional groups began to enter society to find career opportunities blocked by the restricted-access system. By the 1830's, there was widespread lack of confidence in the workings of the 1791 constitution, even among moderate men because the ruling groups, secure behind their prerogative powers, were so unresponsive to assembly criticism. The executive, as established in 1791, was widely distrusted because in William Hamilton Merritt's succinct phrase, it was "beyond the control of the people."[10] Throughout the 1820's and 1830's, executive and assembly were typically at loggerheads. The 1791 constitution, by creating this gulf between executive and assembly, had produced a recipe for political instability.

This separation of executive from the assembly was not tempered by the sensitive or sensible political judgment of governors, for most of them, down to the 1830's, were military men, former officers of the Duke of Wellington. And those who were not, men like Dalhousie in Lower Canada, took strong, authoritarian views of their duties, chief of which were to uphold prerogative power and run their own administration. The reason Sir Francis Bond Head's appointment in 1835 as lieutenant-governor in Upper Canada raised so much hope among Reformers is that he was the first civilian to be chosen for that post. But even Head who, at the time of his appointment was a Poor Law Commissioner for Kent, was a retired officer from the Royal Engineers. Like most lieutenant-governors and governors, he had little knowledge and no experience of parliamentary politics in England and was ill-equipped to promote the kind of cooperation Earl Grey thought essential to the proper working of the British constitution. Nor were prospects enhanced by the fact that the executive councillors acted as individuals rather than as a local version of the British cabinet with its developing characteristic of collective decision-making.

One of the most incisive critiques of the 1791 system, all the more telling because it did not come from a Reformer, was that penned in 1839 by Poulett Thomson, the governor sent out to calm the post-rebellion atmosphere and prepare for whatever major constitutional changes his London masters decided upon as a solution to the troubles in Canada. Thomson was a conservative who considered himself a moderate, suspicious alike of the old, exclusive Toryism and the more forward Reformers, whom he judged to be too democratic. As he assessed the sorry state of affairs in the Canadas, Thomson drew attention to the isolation of the government. "A deeply rooted animosity appears to prevail against a majority of the officers of the Executive Government," he observed, and he went on to emphasize that this animosity was not simply confined to a disgruntled minority. The antagonistic view of the executive was "not confined to the popular party alone but |was| shared extensively by those who claim to be supporters of the Prerogative of the Crown." In his analysis of the defects of the existing constitution, Thomson focused on the paradox that the executive, by British standards, was weak in spite of its dominant position. It was weak because there was no concerted policy-making among the executive. They did not meet regularly as a group to decide what action the government should take on various issues or to assess the state of opinion in the assembly or in the country. There was, wrote Thomson, "a total want of system and power in the executive." Moreover, the executive had no influence in the assembly. There was no minister who could present and explain government-prepared legislation. The executive councillors were not organized to present and guide legislation through the assembly and legislative council. Thomson understood well enough that under the British system, the executive, or the Crown's ministers, had "the duty . . . to initiate and perfect the measures necessary for the good of the country, and, above all, to endeavour to give to the action of those Bodies |the legislative council and the assembly| the direction which will make their labours more efficient. This duty, one of the most important that can devolve on a Government has hitherto been entirely neglected in Canada."[11]

Thomson was drawing attention to the complete absence in the Canadas of the regular relationship between the executive and legislature which made the British constitution work so well. Compared to the normal pattern of administration in Britain, governors and executive councillors had "pursued the opposite course." Instead of trying to manage and work with the assembly, the colonial administration had simply kept functioning in a separate executive sphere. "The local Government," Thomson pointed out, "has not only abstained from taking the initiative in measures of Legislation, but it appears to have studiously repudiated those legitimate means of influence without which it could scarce be carried on." There was never any political leader in the assembly, "authorised or instructed to explain to the House the views of the Government." On top of this lack of influence in the legislature, the government itself was a collection of individual place holders rather than a coherent policy-making group. Executive councillors and department heads did not regard it as necessary to follow the wishes of the governors (as Sir George Arthur noted with surprise in 1839), which meant that government business was conducted by those "five or six individuals in town" who could agree as to public measures. The government of Upper Canada, concluded Thomson, was indeed "a mere clique in the Capital," which had "no influence and attempted to give no direction to their proceedings | in the legislative council and the assembly |." As a consequence of this colonial departure from British norms, "the Executive Government has in great measure lost its legitimate influence over the actions of the Legislature upon matters which have been under their deliberation."[12]

This divergence of the 1791 constitutional system from British practices was regarded by Lord Durham as the root cause of the instability and discord of Canadian politics. In his 1839 report on the rebellions he pointed out, in an incredulous tone, that the assembly had no influence at all on "the nomination of a single servant of the crown."[13] Louis Turcotte, in his account of these years, drew particular attention to conditions in Lower Canada where *le parti anglais* controlled the executive and legislative councils but had no weight or influence in the Canadien-controlled assembly.[14] The local governments in the Canadas then had no systematic relationship with the assemblies, and partly because they did not have to present a coherent, united front on public issues, they were themselves a collection of individuals and cliques. They believed they had no need to manage and influence the assemblies because the 1791 constitution had, up to 1831-32, given them sanction to manage by use of prerogative powers. In Upper Canada, by the 1830's, this meant, as Thomson observed, that the assembly was "in a most disorganised state" because it was a forum for excluded or discontented elements and that "the government has little power in it owing to the want of a system."[15] The assembly of Lower Canada was more organized because of the number and solidarity of the French-Canadian members, but that assembly was in unproductive conflict with government in the 1830's.

In 1850, Lord Elgin, three years into his governorship, attempted a detached and historical assessment of the 1791 constitution to understand why it had been so trouble-prone and had created such unstable political conditions by the 1820's. Under the 1791 constitution, Elgin reasoned, the Canadas continued to exhibit characteristics that had created political difficulties in the American colonies. The system in the thirteen colonies had disintegrated because the assemblies, bedeviled by "country" shibboleths, had "excluded every member of the Cabinet from their legislature." This led to a lack of that co-operation between assemblies and executive that Elgin, like Earl Grey and all other British constitutional experts, believed essential. This failure was typical of countries like France and the United States which, according to Elgin, had weak governments and unstable politics when compared to Britain. In both these countries, there was "so little to secure the cooperation of the Legislative and Executive powers." Indeed, Elgin was convinced that the fatal flaw of the American system, after independence, was the perpetuation of the divide between executive and legislative spheres that had developed in the old colonial system. "The fact is," he concluded, "that the Yankee system is our Old Colonial system, with, in certain cases, the principal of popular election substituted for that of nomination by the Crown." Drawing on his recent gubernatorial experience in Jamaica, a colony still moulded on the old pattern, Elgin illustrated his case by suggesting that "Mr. Fillmore [the U.S. President] stands to his Congress very much in the same relation in which I stood to my Assemblies in Jamaica." The constitutional weakness in Jamaica, in the old thirteen colonies, in the independent United States and in the Canadas after 1791 was "the same absence of effective responsibility in the conduct of legislation—the same want of concurrent action between the parts of the political machine."[16]

Thus, the 1791 constitution, which had been designed to ensure British-style government in the Canadas, turned out to be fundamentally at odds with British constitutional and political custom. Power was exercised by appointed officials and nominated councillors who were not required to respond to concerns among the people or within the assembly. Politicians within the assembly did not conduct themselves in the expectation of receiving office, and because of their permanent exclusion, they became frustrated and characteristically outspoken in their criticisms.[17] The language of politics, by the 1830's, had become violent and extreme. Executive and legislative criticized, challenged, berated, or ignored each other from their separate corners.

If the failure of the 1791 constitution to reproduce the actual working formula of the British constitution was a recipe for political instability, a related and equally profound problem was the disparity between the vision of the 1791 Act and the reality of North American social conditions. In its quest to reproduce British patterns, the 1791 constitution had envisioned the creation of an hereditary landed class, the members of which would sit on the legislative councils. The objective was to build up the councils to the point where they would have the same constitutional, political, and social influence as the House of Lords in England. For the firm establishment of British rather than American political tendencies, it was thought that a superior social class would act as a counterweight to the strong democratic pull of North American society. But this hope proved to be a mirage. Even in the old colony of Quebec, with the remnants of a hierarchical social structure, the members of the seigneurial class had none of the weight or influence needed for this role. British governors thought the seigneurs might constitute the beginnings of such a class, but as Fernand Ouellet has so carefully shown, the seigneurial claim to have influence only masked their growing irrelevance as a group that could mould opinion and organize political support.[18] In Lower Canada, the legislative council became the exclusive preserve of officials of *le parti anglais* and a few French-Canadian collaborators. The council was seen simply as an extension of the executive and had no influence in the community.

Although Tory hopes remained high in Upper Canada from the 1790's to the 1820's, it was clear to any objective observer who studied the legislative councils that the cause was doomed. Lieutenant-Governor Simcoe in the 1790's had talked optimistically of having his hereditary council, but by the 1830's Chief Justice Robinson could only lament that there was "no counteracting influence of an ancient aristocracy, of a great landed interest or even of a wealthy agricultural class."[19] Robinson acknowledged that there were not "in this colony, materials for the formation of a body having the same relative influence as the House of Lords in England."[20] That venerable old loyalist Tory Richard Cartwright complained in the same vein about conditions "where almost universal suffrage prevails, where the great mass of the people are uneducated and where there is little of that salutary influence which hereditary rank and great wealth exercise in Great Britain."[21] Some belated efforts were made in the 1830's to increase the influence of the legislative council by enlarging its size, thus pulling in new members with some status in the community, but it was a fruitless endeavour. As John Macauley, a second generation Loyalist, saw, conditions were too different in Canada and Britain. There "is no country in the world," he conceded, where "materials can be found for a legislative body corresponding in influence with the British House of Peers."[22] Throughout the period since 1791, the legislative councils were composed of officials and lay members who were inclined to support the prerogative power of the executive. They were extensions of officialdom rather than institutions with influence in the country. They added to the political instability of the time because they were yet another target of privilege for the Reformers to aim at. In his characteristically forthright manner, Lord Elgin summed it up in the late 1840's, when he wrote that legislative councillors "were worse than useless . . . they have no weight whatsoever in the community."[23]

Canadian conditions precluded the development of a class functionally equivalent to the British peerage. They also prevented the successful construction of another pillar in the English system, the established Church of England. The prospect of the Anglican church taking any kind of major influence in Catholic Lower Canada outside the English minority was, of course, a dead letter from the start, but in the case of Upper Canada, the framers of the 1791 constitution did plan seriously for the established church to play a central role. The church was supposed to fulfil functions similar to those of the Anglican church in England since 1688. It was to encourage religious uniformity, enable a link to be established between Anglicanism and office-holding, and inculcate respect for the 1791 constitution and the social hierarchy that would naturally emerge. But far from preparing the ground for a stable and deferential society, the church clauses of the 1791 constitution led to increasingly bitter divisions throughout the 1820's, 1830's, and 1840's. The privileges of the Church of England, particularly the granting of clergy reserves, were challenged first by Presbyterians (initially claiming to be an "established" church, too), then by Methodists, Baptists, and the other dissenters. The issue continued to inflame political life until it was settled in 1854, when the most galling Anglican privileges and perquisites were abolished.[24]

The 1791 Act had failed to develop a stable and comprehensive local variant of British structures. The constitution did not work in the way in which Earl Grey described its operation in Britain. Canadian social and economic circumstances ensured that the established church would not survive and revealed the futility of expecting the legislative councils to be like the House of Lords. On all three fronts (constitutional relations between executive and assembly, established church, privileged class), the 1791 legislation had created unworkable options. The chronic instability thus induced combined with the economic and social dislocations of the 1830's to erupt into the armed rebellions in 1837-38.

Although these rebellions were easily suppressed, they did force the British ministers and colonial politicians into an evaluation of why the Canadas had such a troubled record, and all the shortcomings of the 1791 constitution were brought under public scrutiny. Die-hard Tories in the late 1830's might call themselves "the Constitutional Party," but it was clear to all but them that the 1791 constitution would have to be drastically overhauled. The fate of the rebellions had shown that there was no majority support for an American-style solution of becoming independent and starting afresh (although the rebellion in Lower Canada was more popular because of its nationalist aspect). Proposals to introduce many more elective, rather than appointed, officials made considerable appeal in western Upper Canada in the area of William Duncombe's uprising. This was the region most affected by American political culture and, by the 1850's, the heartland of the Grit movement with its love of small government and elected officials.[25] But such solutions as shifting from an appointive to an elective system were not popular among Reformers as a whole. In his idiosyncratic way, William Lyon Mackenzie urged the setting up of an independent, democratic republic in which all privilege and hierarchy would turn to dust, but such proposals never had wide appeal. Neither in Upper nor Lower Canada was the American answer of getting rid of monarchy, writing rules that could contain executive and legislature in their separate spheres, and prescribing rules for their interaction turned to. Given the unpopularity of American ways and the depth of loyalty to Britain, the problem then became how to work out changes that removed the flaws of the 1791 system while staying within British and colonial political and constitutional norms.

The heart of the matter still was how to bring the executive and the assembly into a working relationship that corresponded to the relationship of crown ministers and Parliament in Britain.[26] Some Tories, in a desperate effort to keep as much of their cherished 1791 constitution as intact as possible, proposed some fancy legal and administrative changes.[27] If executive councillors were made impeachable, this would give the assembly some control over executive government. So too would some system of regular administrative reporting or consulting with the assembly. But this Tory solution only gave the assembly last-resort control of councillors and only contemplated the assembly bringing individual officials to account for their policies. It was too little, too late and merely a rearguard action to keep the 1791 system, with all its built-in conflict, in place. Moderate Tories and Reformers alike understood that the 1791 constitution was in shambles and that some structural adjustments would have to be made. In the heated post-rebellion atmosphere, with border raids and fears of American invasion in Upper Canada, with the constitution suspended in Lower Canada, and with the weak British Whig government postponing action until they learned Lord Durham's views and tested parliamentary opinion, no quick action was taken. But with the establishment of the Union of Upper and Lower Canada in 1840-41, British ministers and governors and colonial political leaders had to face the task of working out a new course for politics in Canada.

Bearing in mind the central flaw in the 1791 constitution, it is not surprising that the preoccupation of the Canadian political world during the first years of the Union was how to achieve "harmony" between executive and assembly.[28] The word was on everyone's lips, and it was used again and again during debates on the nature of government questions. Tories, moderate Conservatives, and Reformers disagreed about how it should be achieved. Tories thought in terms of making councillors individually responsible for their actions; moderate Conservatives (such as William Draper) thought in terms of a council, intelligently selected by the governor, able to win the confidence of the assembly; Reformers thought in terms of councillors selected from political leaders who could command a majority within the assembly. Yet, although they disagreed about how this harmony was to be established, all three groups worked to maintain a strong executive with unchecked appointive powers. Contemporaries, even Reformers, talked in terms of achieving harmony so the executive could act effectively on public issues because it would no longer be the creature of closed elites but would be supported by the assembly and, in turn, would be able to use legitimate means of influence to manage majorities in the assembly. All sides were committed to the monarchical system which gave the executive, if it was regarded as legitimate, access to and use of prerogative powers previously exercised by governors on their own. The rebellions had further discredited the prospect of a successful "country" ideology with its penchant for attacking central government and (in its North American version) its insistence on elective control of officials. Tories, moderate Conservatives, and Reformers were all committed to "court"-style government. They differed on how access to that power was to be arranged.

This "court" or "statist" orientation, even among those who were condemned by contemporaries as outright enemies of the 1791 constitution, can be seen most revealingly in the 1839 report of Lord Durham. So much whiggish writing has been done on Durham's concept of responsible government that the context within which he viewed government and politics has often been misrepresented. As he investigated conditions in the Canada, Durham, with his British preconceptions, became convinced that the executive under the 1791 constitution had actually been too weak. It was weak because it had no influence in the assembly or in the country. In both the Canadas, the executive rested on such a narrow and exclusive basis that it was constantly on the defensive, acting in arbitrary ways and deploying patronage in a constant effort to shore itself up. Moreover, since executive councillors tended to act as individuals, there was no coherent approach to public policy, no "administration" in the British sense, ready to bring legislation before the assembly, ready to influence political opinion. Durham's remedy for this state of affairs was for the governor to choose as his advisers politicians who had influence in the assembly and the country and who could, with the governor's co-ordinating powers, act as an entity similar to the British cabinet. All this presupposed a more assertive and extensive use of gubernatorial power, which Durham thought to be necessary and natural. Governors had acted as leaders of cliques instead of making their proper influence felt. "The defective want of administration," he explained, with reference to Lower Canada, "commences at the very source of power; and the efficiency of the public service is impaired throughout by the entire want in the colony of any vigorous administration of the prerogative of the crown."[29]

To achieve more effective government, Durham saw that the governor would have to accept all the ramifications of the presence of elected assemblies, ramifications that governors had ignored since 1791. They should now take into their councils political leaders from the assembly and so be in a position to conduct government business effectively in the legislature. "The crown in Canada," Durham insisted, "would have to submit to the necessary consequence of representative institutions," which meant that administrations would have to be carried on "by means of those in whom the representative body has confidence." This advice of Durham's, that the governors must use political leaders as councillors, is the most familiar, not to say famous, of his arguments, but Durham's starting and finishing points focused on the need to increase executive weight and influence by means of a broader and more vigorous exercise of the governor's powers. "I would not," emphasized Durham, "impair a single prerogative of the Crown; on the contrary, I believe that the interests of the people of these colonies require the protection of prerogatives which have not hitherto been exercised."[30]

The most respected Reform leader among English Canadians during the late 1830's and 1840's concurred in this view that the executive needed strengthening. Robert Baldwin took pains to explain that his proposed changes for the 1791 constitution were not designed to lead to the small, weak central governments in the United States. The reforms "would be accomplished without the least entrenching upon the just and necessary prerogatives of the Crown, which I consider, when administered by the Lieutenant-Governor through the medium of a Provincial ministry responsible to the Provincial Parliament, to be an essential part of the constitution of the province." Even as he refused to take office under Governor Bagot in the Union, Baldwin reiterated that he wished "to see a strong Government established, not one like those in the neighboring states blown about by every wind and bowing before every storm, but one that anchored in the affections of the people would be enabled to ride triumphantly over every adverse wave."[31]

Both Durham and Baldwin, then, although committed to changing the 1791 constitution, were convinced that the executive would have to be made stronger and more influential. This is a cardinal point the significance of which is often underestimated. Because the old ruling elites in Upper and Lower Canada were unchecked by assemblies and acted arbitrarily, they appeared to be powerful, but, in fact, they were too narrow to have an effective reach in society. Because they were vulnerable, they reacted testily and fearfully to reform critics. Durham and Baldwin wished to adopt solutions that would not leave government weak in society, with the possibility of an American pattern evolving in which a weak executive confronted a strong popular assembly. However, while they agreed on the need to encourage a British-style executive, Durham and Baldwin differed on how to achieve that end. Durham emphasized the role of the governor as the co-ordinator and initiator of public policy, based on the advice of well-chosen councillors; Baldwin emphasized the role of the councillors, envisioning that these political leaders should become the real controllers of the administration.

It was on these differing interpretations of responsible government that the political debate between 1840 and 1849 turned. The central issue revolved around the role of the governor, whether he was to be an active political force or begin to become only a figurehead. It was an issue that deeply

divided contemporaries, especially when it is understood that even Reformers had qualms about reducing the Crown's power and status in Canada. In
addition to these genuine doubts about the fate of the governor, there were
other important crosscurrents stirring the complex and heated political
atmosphere of the 1840's.

First, there were many Tories who interpreted any continuing gubernatorial co-ordinating role as a means of keeping the old system as intact as
possible. Thus, when governors like Sydenham and Metcalfe took on such a
commanding role between 1840 and 1844, they were supported partly by
moderates, who saw this in the post-Durham context of modified reform, but
also by outright Tories, who wished little movement towards political
co-operation between governor and popular leaders. On the Reform side,
there was a deep distrust of all governors because men in that office since
1791 had always acted as Tory partisans. So the clear difference emphasized
between Baldwin and Durham on the role of the governor was complicated
by Tory hopes and Reform distrust.[32]

The second important complicating factor was the nationalism of the
French Canadians. Once the Union was in place and representative institutions re-established, the French Canadians, led by LaFontaine, wished to use
their electoral dominance in Lower Canada to regain their language rights
and prevent enactment of further assimilative policies. Thus, whereas a
Reform leader like Baldwin from Canada West might be prepared to work
with a sympathetic governor, LaFontaine and his followers would not enter
any administration until given assurances on the language issue and on the
right of French Canadians to gain their natural weight in colonial administration.[33] The solidarity of the French-Canadian electorate had a great impact
on the nature and timing of responsible government in Canada.

A third factor contributing to the continuing instability and complexity
was the absence of any written formula to explain the way in which the
relationship between executive and Parliament was successfully worked in
Britain. As the colonial reformer Edward Gibbon Wakefield remarked, in
the British working constitution "the sole guarantee was usage."[34] The big
problem, as it had been throughout the colonies during the eighteenth
century, was how to implement British practices when these were not
written down and were, indeed, an evolving process rooted in British social,
legal, and political conditions.

It is instructive to bear in mind that in Britain as late as 1834, William IV
still believed he had the prerogative power to ask Robert Peel to form an
administration in spite of his weak position in the Commons.[35] Throughout
the 1830's and 1840's, many leading British Tories, including enlightened
ones like Peel, believed it was important to protect, with all its ramifications,
the concept of "his majesty's government" and shore up the House of Lords

and Church of England.[36] And even though majority control in the Commons was essential for any government's survival after 1832, most cabinet ministers still came from the non-elected upper chamber. Because of the piecemeal, evolutionary development of the British constitution and because there existed no codification of how ministers were to get on with the Commons, there was ample room for disagreement about how to introduce British practices into Canada. A major attempt was made during the first session of the Union assembly to put down in writing the procedures for achieving the generally desired harmony between executive and assembly. But these so-called "responsible government resolutions" of 1841 failed to meet the case because it was difficult to write down all the assumptions and customs in the British practice and because the Reformers' had a deep distrust of the governor's commitment to establish a regular and open relationship with the assembly.[37]

The root difficulty was not that the governors between 1840 and 1844 were reactionary but that they had a different version of responsible government, a version they believed better guaranteed the preservation of the monarchical constitution in Canada. Governors like Sydenham and Metcalfe genuinely thought that the system they were trying to introduce at the top of the power structure reflected the kind of changes recommended by Durham. Remember that Durham had written of the need to strengthen the executive and extend the influence of prerogative power. This would be quite legitimate if the governor chose as his advisers men with political standing in the colony. Sydenham, the first governor in the Union, had made a trenchant critique of the 1791 system of rule by cliques and was fully committed to working with more popular councillors. Sir George Arthur, the last lieutenant-governor of Upper Canada, forecast, when exchanging views with the future governor of the Union, that the new governor would endeavour "to make the Executive far more influential and consequently far more responsible."[38] In one of his early despatches to Lord John Russell, Sydenham explained his approach. There was, he wrote, a need for "a more vigorous and efficient system of Government . . . which conducted in harmony with the wishes of the People, will, at the same time, be enabled to give direction to the popular Branch of the Legislature."[39] The task of the governor was to choose councillors with some influence, use their advice to prepare coherent public policies, and employ the combined influence of the council to work legislation through the assembly. In all this, the governor was to take the initiative, functioning almost as a prime minister.[40] Metcalfe, in particular, believed that in pursuing such a course, he was, in fact, implementing some of Durham's proposals. The colonial reformers in Britain certainly believed he was essentially right. Metcalfe's stubborn response to Baldwin and LaFontaine was based on his conviction that he *was* practising responsible government.[41]

There were enough sympathetic and co-operative political leaders about to make the governors think this approach had a reasonable chance of success. None of the governors relied on the old compact Tories because that group was still wedded to pre-1837 ways and it was too narrow to have influence wide enough to be of help to the executive. There were moderate Tories, however, who understood that there could be no return to the unreconstructed 1791 constitution. This moderation was best exemplified in the person of William Draper, the political mentor of the young John A. Macdonald. Draper agreed that the governor should choose advisers from beyond the former ruling elites, but he also held that the governor should remain the centre of gravity within the administration.[42] From Canada East such a prominent figure as Denis Benjamin Viger, a former knowledgeable and persistent critic of the Chateau Clique, was prepared to work with the governor on such terms.[43] The sticking point was that not enough of the political leaders were so disposed. Above all, the two most influential Reform leaders, LaFontaine and Baldwin, had deep misgivings about leaving so much initiative and so much room for manoeuvre to the governor. If the governor listened to the advice of his politician-councillors but was not bound to take that advice, and if the governor remained as the controlling force in administration, then the Reform leaders feared a perpetuation of the old ways. Ever since 1791, the governors had seemed to act as Tory partisans; they could not now be trusted to act impartially. Moreover, the whole apparatus of government, built up since 1791 by Tory and gubernatorial patronage, was loaded against the Reformers. It was essential, therefore, as the Reform leaders learned their lessons from past experience, that the governor yield up more weight and more initiative to the popular political leaders who ought to be chosen to sit on the council. Only in this way could the old, exclusive system finally be opened up.

It was the existence of these two differing approaches to more responsible government that caused the crisis during Metcalfe's governorship in 1844. The feelings on both sides were so bitter because both sides believed they possessed an enlightened understanding of how responsible government should work. Metcalfe, Draper, and Viger were absolutely convinced they had given up the old ways; LaFontaine and Baldwin insisted the governor's role would have to be reduced even more. The crisis began in an entirely characteristic fashion when Metcalfe dismissed LaFontaine and Baldwin on the grounds they wished to reduce the governor's power on administration patronage.

This "famous and much misrepresented controversy," as Egerton Ryerson, the Methodist leader and erstwhile Reformer, characterized it, was about the remaining power of the royal prerogative, as exercised by the governor, in Canada.[44] A.D. Harvey has argued that the real key to political conflict in the early part of the nineteenth century in Britain was not reform or reaction but the issue of the royal prerogative,[45] and a good case can be made that this was still true in Canada between 1840 and 1849. It was certainly at the centre of the Metcalfe controversy. The way in which contemporaries divided in the crisis is puzzling if the issue of the prerogative is not brought to the forefront. The fact that Denis Benjamin Viger, the old critic of executive tyranny in Lower Canada, supported Metcalfe "parait extraordinaire" to Louis Turcotte.[46] But Metcalfe was also treated with some sympathy by Papineau and Nielson, former rebels against the Crown; by MacNab, the Tory chief from Upper Canada; by the colonial reformer, Wakefield; and by the liberal-minded Methodist leader Egerton Ryerson. Explanations have been offered by scholars to explain this curious mixture of support to the effect that Viger wanted office, Ryerson wanted to be superintendent of education, and that Wakefield hoped to get some consideration for his Beauharnois canal scheme.[47] All this may be true, but such propositions should not obscure the fact that there was a genuine constitutional issue here, the question of the royal prerogative, an issue that even in the more stable and homogeneous British setting had troubled contemporaries between 1800 and 1840.

Let us look at Metcalfe's case. He believed, with considerable justification, that he was following the course suggested by Durham in attempting to govern efficiently and vigorously by appointing to this council and consulting leading politicians from the assembly. Colonial reformers in Britain saw nothing wrong with Metcalfe's behaviour. According to the *Colonial Gazette*, Metcalfe had "governed Canada by the constitution he found there. He had the right to dismiss his councillors; he has a right to endeavour to procure new ones; the only limit to the time allowed him for doing this is the necessity of assembling the Provincial Parliament as soon as some constitutional function, which it alone is competent to discharge, requires to be discharged."[48] As J.M.S. Careless has shown, both Metcalfe and Lord Stanley believed it important for the working of the Union constitution to preserve the Crown's prerogative.[49] This was not a reactionary view to take when Lord Durham's analysis is borne in mind. In his instructions to Metcalfe, Lord Stanley had explained that the governor was to consult his councillors and "pay due deference to their advice," but he was to remember that "you yourself [are] the head of your administration, not even bound to adopt their advice, although always bound to receive it." There was nothing in these instructions that ran counter to the views of Durham and other colonial reformers. Wakefield had written to LaFontaine on learning of Metcalfe's initial appointment that Canada had "the perfect Governor-General," and his support of Metcalfe through the crisis was consistent with his view that the governor should exercise superiority and management over his advisers. In this view of the issue, for Metcalfe to give into LaFontaine and Baldwin would be "the virtual surrender into the hands of the council of the prerogative of the Crown."[50]

Metcalfe was convinced, from the time he arrived in Canada, that his Reform councillors were bent on attacking this prerogative power—there was, from the beginning, "an antagonism between his views and those of his ministers on the subject of the prerogative." Submission to his councillors on the patronage issue would mean that the governor was "solely and completely a tool in the hands of the Council" unable to "have any exercise of his own judgment in the administration of the Government." In so reasoning, Metcalfe was thinking with concepts of the old colonial system as amended by critics in the aftermath of the rebellions. He still saw individual councillors as responsible for their own departments and as individual sources of advice, except that since 1840, these councillors had been appointed partly on the basis of their political weight in the country. But still, like Durham and Wakefield, he did not envisage the council as equivalent in composition and function to the British cabinet. "The Council," complained Metcalfe, "are now spoken of by themselves and others generally as 'the Ministers,' 'the Administration,' 'the Cabinet,' 'the Government' and so forth. Their pretensions are according to this new nomenclature. They . . . expect that the policy and conduct of the governor shall be subservient to their views and party purposes."[51]

If we remember the range of Metcalfe's supporters, it is clear that his position was plausible. The response of Egerton Ryerson is revealing for it brings out many of the nuances that troubled contemporaries. At the outset, Ryerson supported the councillors against the governor, but the closer he studied the issue and English practices, the more he was convinced that "the question of the prerogative" was involved and that it was important to prevent the governor becoming a mere "recorder" for prior decisions made by council members. He was particularly disturbed by what he believed to be an effort by LaFontaine and Baldwin to extract a written declaration from Metcalfe that he would not make any appointments without consulting them. If things were to work that way, it would mean that Queen Victoria would have no right to resist Robert Peel if he put up Daniel O'Connell for a peerage. "It is an essential principle," believed Ryerson, "that in the British Constitution the crown should be free, should be undefined in its prerogative. The exercise of that prerogative may be checked in various ways but to bind it by promises is to infringe its constitutional liberty." To deflect criticism that he had betrayed his "ultra-liberal" record, Ryerson pointed out his consistency on this matter since he had supported Head, Arthur, and Sydenham from 1836 to 1841 in their gubernatorial exercise of the crown prerogative.[52]

The other revealing response to the crisis was that of Viger, which Turcotte thought so extraordinary. It is now so much a piece of received wisdom that Metcalfe opposed responsible government that it is quite startling to learn of Viger's view that "le peuple devait l'octroi du gouvernement responsable en Canada à Lord Metcalfe."[53] Viger's case rested on the grounds that Metcalfe deserved all the credit for the quick return of the exiled 1837 patriots, that Metcalfe had actively supported the Draper and Viger effort to end proscription of the French language in the Union, and that Metcalfe tried manfully to include respectable leaders of the French-Canadian community (such as Viger himself and Papineau) to serve as his advisers. Viger further believed that under such a system of prominent French Canadians working with the governor, it would be possible to protect French Canadians from assimilation. It seemed a much more straightforward solution than LaFontaine's course of making party alliances with the suspect protestant democracy of Upper Canada, a marriage of convenience that Viger did not think could be a permanent solution for French Canadians.[54] Viger was an old man by 1843; his views were old-fashioned, and he lost many of his listeners when he indulged in long disquisitions on parliamentary usage. In the end, he failed because he could not command any significant electoral support. But his failure was not inevitable. It was only LaFontaine's remarkable ability to discipline and hold his electoral support that prevented Metcalfe, Viger, and Draper putting into place a legitimate conservative version of responsible government.

LaFontaine and the French-Canadian voters who stood by him were the key to how the crisis of 1843-44 worked out and the key to the version of responsible government that finally emerged. Metcalfe's position did have constitutional sanction behind it. As Wakefield knowledgeably argued, if the governor entered into a pledge about patronage or any other major administrative matter, "he would openly divest the Crown of its acknowledged prerogative, degrade the royal office into obvious and proclaimed subordination to the Executive Council and more seriously impair the constitution which it is the glory of this Province to possess."[55] Tory leaders like MacNab and moderate Conservative leaders like Draper still accepted the need for a strong governor; many Reform leaders such as Ryerson and Baldwin had agreed at various times that, providing the council was chosen from local notables outside the old cliques, the governor should remain the centre of the administration. Durham had sketched out such a system in his report; prominent French-Canadian leaders like Viger were prepared to work on these terms. It even seemed, for a time, that Papineau returning from exile might be asked to join the council. In the end, it was the solidarity of French-Canadian support for LaFontaine that broke the Metcalfe strategy.

LaFontaine understood this well. Under the old system, the assembly had possessed no influence on government, but now that the governors were seeking popular support, the French Canadians were in a commanding position because of "the confidence which they place in their public men."[56] To dissipate this strength, to allow Viger and other patrician figures to have equal influence with LaFontaine would only enable the governor to ignore party and lead to a reversion "to the old system of government— viz: the will of the Governor."[57] It was the French-Canadian fact, with its ability to produce a majority party, that determined when responsible government came it would be party-government and not governor-government. The French-Canadian presence was obviously the feature that most distinguished Canadian from British conditions. It was this fact that enabled the political party of the Reformers to make such decisive claims on the Crown's prerogative powers in Canada. As M. Errol Bouchette observed, "in reading the history of our first fifty years of constitutional struggles, one is struck by the great power of the French-Canadian electorate." |"En lisant l'histoire de nos cinquantes premieres années de lutte constitutionelle, on est frappé du calme plein de puissance de l'électorat Canadien."| He concluded provocatively but accurately, "responsible government was the work of French Canadians." |"Le gouvernement responsable est l'oeuvre des Canadiens."|[58]

The pressures generated by the heated debates of the 1830's and 1840's, culminating in the Metcalfe crisis of 1843-44, had longlasting consequences on Canadian political values, assumptions, and structures. A shift of major significance was the transfer of gubernatorial prerogative powers to political leaders. The function of governors in the Union was surrounded by ambiguity. While representing the Crown and selected for office by the British cabinet, they viewed themselves and were viewed by British ministers between 1840 and 1846 as the active leaders of the Canadian administration. This meant that the governor was acting as king and prime minister at the same time, a blending of functions that led to some extraordinary actions as governors used what they deemed to be legitimate prerogative powers to shore up their political position as "prime minister." During the first general election in the Union, for example, Sydenham worked in an avowedly partisan manner in actual electoral management, using his gubernatorial influence and powers to undermine opponents. By royal proclamation, Sydenham altered electoral boundaries in Canada East in a plan to favour English and urban districts which would vote for administration candidates. In LaFontaine's own constituency at Terrebonne, the polling place was moved to the Scots and Irish settlement of New Glasgow in preparation for organized intimidation of French-Canadian voters who would support LaFontaine and the Reform cause.

Sydenham's goal was to break up political parties in the country, particularly the solid support that LaFontaine held in Canada East. Once that party strength had been broken, the governor could then deal with political leaders in the assembly as individuals, thus "keeping the whole conduct of the executive government in his own hands,"[59] With this kind of electoral manipulation taking place in the name of the Crown and with the constitutional and racial issues at stake in the new Union, the 1841 election was the most bitter and disorderly contemporaries could remember. Sydenham relished the struggle. "The governor plans and talks of nothing else," noted T.W.C. Murdoch, his civil secretary. The tactics Sydenham adopted were, he believed, a legitimate exercise of his gubernatorial rights. "I fought the whole battle myself," Sydenham wrote triumphantly in June 1841.[60] While Sydenham may have been more thorough and foresighted in thus using his prerogative powers to manipulate elections, governors under the 1791 constitution had always regarded such activities as legitimate, especially in times of crisis. In the tumultuous 1836 election in Upper Canada, Sir Francis Bond Head had made firm use of his power to disqualify potential Reform voters.[61]

Electoral manipulation by the executive entered Canadian political culture not because of French Canadian unfamiliarity with democracy and a consequent readiness to abuse it, but because of the assumptions and activities of the British governors such as Head and Sydenham. When, beginning with Elgin, these gubernatorial powers were suspended, they were not discarded but were taken over, with their aura of legitimacy, by the Canadian politicians. Macdonald's easy justification of the 1882 gerrymander and the 1885 franchise legislation are fine examples of this Canadian political mentality. Electoral manipulation by the executive was firmly embedded in Canadian political culture during the 1840's.

A related feature of the Canadian political landscape was also formed by the 1840's—executive use of patronage to maintain and strengthen party support for the administration. The use of patronage , as we have seen, had deep roots in Canada; the Family Compact and the Chateau Clique in Upper and Lower Canada had relied on executive patronage to build up their network of support in the localities. With the demise of the 1791 system, patronage lost none of its importance. In the Union, the governors needed to build support in the assembly if they wished to continue as active heads of administration, the alternative being domination by whichever political group was able to control the assembly. For their part, the Reform leaders of the 1840's knew how critical it was for their purposes to gain access to patronage. Neither LaFontaine nor Baldwin were democrats. Some critics, in fact, thought LaFontaine took on too many aristocratic airs in public, and Elgin perceptively noted that Baldwin was "the most Conservative public man in Upper Canada."[62] They did not, then, wish to destroy the monarchical system with its appointive rather than elective methods of running the country. They simply wished to open up the system, break down the power of the narrow elites, and give power and influence to elected leaders who had wider support in the country. They understood that by merely entering the council as individuals, they had made only a small dent in changing an administrative structure that had grown up during decades of Tory patronage distribution. It was of great importance to LaFontaine and Baldwin that the whole range of government appointments should be opened up to their Reform supporters, for only such a basic change would show that the old, restrictive ways had been broken down. Thus in a characteristic Canadian fashion, the great clash of 1843-44 between Governor Metcalfe and his two Reform council members had erupted over the issue of patronage.[63]

Metcalfe refused to allow LaFontaine and Baldwin the extensive influence over appointments they believed essential. If Metcalfe did not take their advice on appointments, if he kept his own counsel or sought advice from individuals outside the council, then the Reform leaders believed their office-holding would be in vain. Their presence would simply validate a covert continuation of the old ways. But once Metcalfe had decided to stick to his guns and fight LaFontaine and Baldwin on this issue, he was driven to throw all his weight behind Draper and Viger in the hope of making them strong enough politically to sustain an administration. Metcalfe became an active partisan; he "constituted himself head of a Party" and "entered himself into the political arena to defend his conduct and win support for his party" | "descendit lui-même dans l'arène politique pour défendre sa conduite et gagner des partisans." |[64] Partly because of his painful illness, but essentially because of these political imperatives, Metcalfe allowed Draper comprehensive use of patronage to strengthen his support. He thus granted to Draper what he had denied to LaFontaine and Baldwin. As Elgin later observed, Draper and the Conservative councillors not only "assented to that claim . . . to dispense the patronage of the crown but acted upon it to the full and unreservedly."[65] When the Reform leaders forced their way back into office by means of their electoral strength, they, in turn, considered it entirely legitimate to distribute patronage to their supporters as a way of maintaining party organization and morale and as a necessary means of destroying the elaborate structure of the 1791 system of privilege. The dialectic of Canadian politics had again determined that patronage remain on centre stage. The configuration of the political battles of the 1840's had "introduced party appointments as an essential feature of responsible government."[66] Thrust aside by developments since 1837, the old Tory remnants lamented this new and (for them) far too comprehensive distribution of patronage. "Till we had responsible government in the colony," despaired that disappointed Tory John Strachan, "we knew nothing of the corruption of government. Now the ministry, as they call it, whether Conservative or Reform seem to have no other object than to get good places. All is party and I may say all is corruption and it matters not which faction is in power."[67]

It was in these conditions of the 1840's that the national political parties of nineteenth-century Canada began to take shape. The Conservative party that was in power for most of the second half of the century coalesced in 1854 as an alliance of Conservatives and moderate Reformers (especially Reformers in French-Canadian Canada East who had achieved their goals and now sought to preserve their language, culture and church). The ideology that the party found serviceable for the rest of the century—an ideology resting on the British connection and monarchical institutions—was in place by 1850.[68] These parties, like the Canadian constitution, were moulded by circumstances into parties that were quite different from the parties of Victorian Britain. Egerton Ryerson was struck by the fact that, although political parties had existed in Britain since 1688, Canadian conditions had produced, by the 1840's, "a distinctive Canadian sense of the term party."[69] When making comparisons between Britain and Canada, British governors complained about "the system of Party Government" in Canada.[70] Although parties existed in Britain, competed for power, and provided majority support for administrations, these British observers, sitting right at the centre of the Canadian political landscape, believed there was something significantly different about Canadian parties and government.

The difference, complained of by Ryerson and remarked on by Elgin (and later, Dufferin) lay in the composition of parties and their reach and influence throughout the social structure. In the British setting although precursors of modern parties within Parliament can be traced from the 1760's onwards, the ramifications of party "extended only a little way into society as a whole."[71] The passing of the 1832 Reform Act increased the size of the political nation and made parties much more important inside and outside Parliament. Political leaders in Parliament now had to pay much more attention to the constituencies, to keep activists at work, to raise funds, to conduct canvasses, to select candidates, and to fight elections. Much of this new and more systematic party work was supervised by agents operating from the Carlton and Reform Clubs. Robert Peel, leader of the Conservative party in the Commons between 1832 and 1846, was particularly acute in seeing the changed context.[72] But even for leaders like Peel, party was seen "essentially as a tool of management" for raising majorities in parliament to enable ministers of the Crown to govern.[73] The British electorate after 1832 was still restricted, certainly compared to the Canadian one. The Church of England and the House of Lords were still powerful influences on political opinion, and leadership within both the Tory-Conservative and Whig-Liberal parties came from a restricted social class which believed it had a natural right to govern. While it was essential to organize in the constituencies, it never occurred to leaders like Peel and Russell that men thrown up by mere popularity in the constituencies should become part of the group from whom ministers were selected. As Walter Bagehot observed of the Victorian constitution, it worked because "the mass of the people yielded obedience to the select few."[74]

Thus, in England, party was a technique of management used by parliamentary leaders from the aristocracy and upper classes. In a two-volume study of English political leaders published in 1859, Daniel Maddyn described the characteristics of party in the English setting. He emphasized that party was one of the glories of the English constitution because it was the vehicle which permitted peaceful changeover of governments. However, he cautioned that while "party should be a habit in Parliament, it does not follow that society should desire that party interests should be eagerly pursued out of doors." Maddyn thought it a distinguishing aspect of the English monarchical constitution that party was restricted in its social repercussions, for an extensive party system throughout society would create conditions of pure democracy that would lead to the weak government and constant political turmoil of the United States. Thus "because the British constitution is a representative form of government it is right that there should be party in Parliament but because England is not ruled by a delegative Democracy it is also right to distrust excess of party spirit out of doors."[75] It was this "excess of party spirit" that British governors found so disturbing in Canada.

In Canada, parties became much more pervasive in their influence, and their reach extended into all corners of society. In contrast to Britain, there was no traditional ruling class (although the framers of the 1791 constitution had hoped one would emerge), there was a much wider franchise, there was a much narrower range of social class, and there was no equivalent to the deference Bagehot believed lay at the foundation of British practices. Moreover, parties in Canada had to be formed quickly in the 1840's. Political leaders like Draper who tended to follow a British-style pattern with an emphasis on party within the assembly found themselves in a weak position. Draper had a kind of aristocratic fastidiousness against building up party in the constituencies. Yet because of the powerful presence of the French-Canadian electorate and because of the need to hold a majority in the assembly in order to gain power, it became clear that systematic and comprehensive party organization had become part of the Canadian political game. Draper did not understand this, but the young John A. Macdonald did. Macdonald saw clearly that the great weakness of the Tory cause in the early 1840's was that it was weak in terms of voter support. The old Tories had no "organisation" in the country.[76] Leaders like Draper still placed too much weight on the ability of the governor to remain the political fount of power and influence. Macdonald saw that the weight had shifted to the constituencies. His profound appreciation of the place of party in Canada was to bring him many years of political success and power.

Canadian society was much more democratic, less disciplined by class and deference, and more geographically dispersed than British society,[77] and so party leaders had to evolve new methods of party-building. In such an unstructured society, any organized segment that could use its resources and network of contacts to support a party became important. The churches in Canada, therefore, became from the outset close collaborators with the party leaders as politicians turned to bishops, priests, ministers, and notable laymen in the localities to promote the cause. Organizations such as the Masons and the Orange Order served similar purposes.[78] In addition to turning to such organizations, political leaders used all the patronage at their disposal to build up party morale and strength. Every appointment, no matter how big or small, was distributed on a partisan basis. It was such aspects of partisanship, reaching into all corners of society, that led Ryerson to write darkly of "the evils of partyism in government" and British governors to believe a different type of "party government" had emerged in Canada.

One other trend intensified the pervasiveness of partisanship in Canada. Between 1791 and 1837, the executive had little need to respond to its critics in the assembly. These critics had no expectation of moving into office in the manner of political opposition leaders in Britain. There was then, from the beginning, a trend for those with no hope of office and no means to call governments to account to become habitually outspoken. The leaders of the disaffected groups "by that habit which is second nature, are demogogues rather than politicians." For their part, the Tory elites, secure from constitutional removal, freely abused the opposition as disloyal and traitorous. In the aftermath of the rebellions, feelings became even more embittered and charges and countercharges more outspoken. Lieutenant-Governor Thomson noted that charges of treason were "unsparingly levelled against a large proportion of the people."[79] When Lord Elgin arrived in Canada in 1847, he found the language between government and opposition to be "incredible in its vindictiveness." Elgin believed the root cause to have been the long years of entrenched executive versus powerless assembly which had led to a pattern where "to revile the one was the surest test of Patriotism—to denounce the other, of Loyalty."[80] The pattern laid down between 1791 and the 1840's continued to affect the nature of parties in Canada. In 1874, Dufferin was discouraged that "party spirit runs so high and is so unscrupulous."[81] Conservative party pamphlets described the Liberal's policy of the 1870's as "veiled treason," and the loyalty cry was at the centre of the 1891 election when Macdonald, that most successful political entrepreneur born of the 1840's, ran in his last election. [82]

Because party strength was so important in the 1840's, because of the urgent need to build up party out of doors and keep supporters loyal, because of the patronage rewards to be gained by active partisanship, and because of the long history of exaggerated language directed at opponents, Canadian parties became, for leaders and supporters alike, much more than tools of political management for leaders in the assembly. Parties became great social institutions. They provided jobs, they functioned as clubs, they served like churches as focal points of faith and loyalty, and they became respected and revered organizations for those who belonged. They acted as an integrating force in a colonial society with no hard and fast symbols of national unity. Donald Creighton catches this important social role of party when he describes so movingly the political picnic grounds in Ontario during the 1870's. From their factional and fragmented origins in the 1840's, the parties were to become grand sacred institutions with branches throughout the towns and countryside of Victorian Canada.[83]

By the middle of the 1850's, the last vestiges of the old 1791 constitutional system had disappeared. The seven-year governorship of Lord Elgin, from 1847 to 1854, determined once and for all that the governor would not be the active head of administration in the manner conceived of by Sydenham and Metcalfe. The governor could still have an important political impact at critical moments, as the "double shuffle" affair of 1858 and the King-Byng episode as late as 1926 demonstrated, but governors from 1847 onwards never acted as leaders of the administration as they had done from Dorchester and Simcoe to Metcalfe between 1791 and 1844. In 1844, as we have seen, Metcalfe could still be surprised by the "new nomenclature" which styled his councillors "the Ministers," "the Administration," "the Cabinet," "the Government" with the consequent expectation that "the policy and conduct of the governor shall be subservient to their views and party purposes." By Elgin's governorship, that new nomenclature described reality. All that was left to the governor was what Elgin referred to as "moral influence," which he naively and mistakenly hoped might "go far to compensate for the loss of power consequent on the surrender of patronage to an executive responsible to the local parliament."[84] The governorship remained as an essential symbol of the British connection and as a guarantor of the monarchical system of government with its appointive rather than elective basis. By 1855, legislation had done away with the clergy reserves and the privileged position of the Anglican church, the seigneurial system of land tenure in Canada East, and with the appointed legislative council. Thus all the expectations and hopes of the 1791 constitution-makers and the Tory elites of Upper and Lower Canada—the evolution of a hereditary class equivalent to the peerage, the setting up of an influential, established church, the creation of "national" ruling class revolving round the governor—had become dimly remembered shadows.

The manner and timing of their going had a profound impact on Canadian political culture. Canadian concepts of the nature and extent of executive power and on the nature and function of parties were moulded during this heated formative period. Canadian political leaders not only assumed executive power because of the strength derived from party position in the assembly, they also took over prerogative powers that had been exercised by the governors ever since 1791. They appointed only their own supporters to posts throughout the public service; they manipulated elections and fell easily into designating the opposition as disloyal and traitorous. They also kept power in their own hands as much as possible for, like the governors, they intended to be the controlling leaders of administration. Thus Macdonald, throughout his long years in power, paid extraordinary attention to the smallest details of patronage and party matters. Macdonald did everything himself in much the same way that Sydenham did everything himself. The characteristic Canadian pattern was set in motion of power being exercised and party held together by a dominant leader keeping nearly all the strings in his hands.

Measured against British and American patterns by the 1850's, Canada's constitution and political culture was emphatically "court" or statist in orientation. On the party leader in power devolved all the appointive rights previously exercised by the governor. The party upon which the leader depended need only to control one chamber to claim exclusive right to all crown appointments. As Macdonald was to say by 1871, this was the true constitutional principle in Canada, that all government posts belonged to party supporters.[85] Had Canada been an ethnically homogeneous colony with a fairly stable population, the "court" might have triumphed completely, but there were important countervailing forces at work that limited the untrammelled growth of central power. French Canadians had sound reasons for voting in a party that would protect their church and culture and would give them jobs, but they did not wish to see a strong central government intervening in their heartland. English Canadians living in the small towns and farms west of Toronto exhibited strong localistic tendencies characteristic of North American agrarian communities in the nineteenth century. Thus, while all the great constitutional issues had been settled by the mid-1850's, the new politics had not yet produced stability. Just as the 1688 revolution in England had failed to create political stability, so the coming of responsible government in Canada needed another twenty years before the emergence of equipoise.

3

STABILITY, 1864-1914

The complexity of Canadian conditions caused continuing political instability even after responsible government and its consequences had solved the constitutional and church establishment questions. The basic problem was the inability of one party to achieve a dominant position. The 1854 alliance of Canada West Conservatives and Tories, Canada East Conservatives and moderate Reformers from both sections (that became the Conservative party) seemed to presage the emergence of one commanding party, but its growth was checked by the peculiar framework of the Union. Each section was assigned permanently 42 and (after 1854) 65 seats in the legislature, but throughout the 1840's and 1850's, immigration increased the English population in Canada West to the point where the opposition in Canada West was able to make a popular claim that they were underrepresented and that government was being unfairly dominated by French Canadians. The "representation by population" cry gave new life to the Reform rump (now calling themselves the Grits because they had stuck to Reform principles) in Canada West and began eating away at the position of the Canada West Conservatives. The potentially powerful new Conservative party could only barely hang on to its majority position for most of the decade from 1854 to 1864. Union and responsible government had led to a partisan deadlock rather than stability. As W.L. Morton has reminded us "instability was the essence of Canadian politics" in the late 1850's and early 1860's.[1] Stability was only to be achieved when the restrictive Union framework was abolished and Confederation created a much broader context within which party-building could take place. After 1867, the Conservative party of Macdonald was able to achieve supremacy as the Whig oligarchy had done in England after 1714. As in eighteenth-century England, so in nineteenth-century Canada, the development of a dominant party turned out to be a necessary condition for political stability.

As J.H. Plumb has pointed out in his acclaimed study of the conditions which led to such stability in England, the reasons for its emergence are too infrequently analyzed by historians. Interest and emphasis tend to focus on instability and change, on radical shifts in social or economic patterns. There is, advises Plumb, a genuine case to be made for understanding why stability develops in a polity.[2] While Plumb's observations may have been made to be fruitfully provocative, it is a profound question to ask about Canada in the middle decades of the nineteenth century. In the 1830's and 1840's, the Canadas were in a continuing state of crisis. Even fellow British North American colonists in Nova Scotia were appalled by the turbulent and divisive politics of these colonies.[3] Yet by the 1870's and 1880's, Canada had achieved political stability and had become the biggest, wealthiest, and most important settlement colony in Victoria's empire.

What had happened to bring about this transformation? The establishing of Confederation in 1867 was clearly an essential pre-condition, but merely joining the colonies together was not, in itself, any guarantee of stability, as the experience of the Union of the Canadas had already shown. In its early years, indeed, Confederation brought in its train a new set of complicating and unsettling factors. The Maritime Provinces were deeply distrustful of the Canadian-controlled state, British Columbia was soon at odds with Ottawa governments on the railway issue, and the federal government floundered over Métis and French language rights in the new Northwest Territory acquired from the Hudson's Bay Company, a matter which added yet another dimension to mistrust between English and French Canadians in Ontario and Quebec. The new Dominion's relationship to Great Britain, from the Washington treaty of 1871 right through to the naval question of 1908-10, had divisive repercussions in Canada. Confederation offered a solution to the political deadlock in the Union (as to a number of other problems facing Britain and her remaining North American colonies in the 1860's), but it also introduced new problems of its own. What Confederation did do, however, was to provide an enlarged context in which other long-term structural changes could take place. Above all, Confederation provided room for the development of political parties that could hold majorities in Parliament and form governments that could stay in office and wield effective power over a long span of years.

The chronic instability in the Canadas had been caused by two basic factors. At the root of the problem initially was the attempt of restricted ruling classes to maintain their power and privileges by formulating their peculiar local version of the British constitution, a version which gave them unchecked control of the executive and its patronage. The attempt eventually failed, but it had led to years of bitter turmoil as opponents mounted incessant attacks on the exclusive system. Second, instability continued after the Union was established and into the 1850's, even when responsible government was in place because no political party operating in the new conditions where the power of the electorate rather than the power of the governor was the key factor could build up a decisive and durable majority position. In the first half of the 1840's, it had been expected that the governors could be a source of stability, and if such a politically sensitive governor as Sydenham (1839-41) had enjoyed a long tenure in office, such a pattern might have taken hold. But in spite of their high-minded constitutional intentions, the governors were regarded as Tory sympathizers, and in 1844 Metcalfe ended up as an apparent Tory partisan. His efforts to make the governorship into a stabilizing force had disastrous consequences for the office. After Metcalfe's complete failure, it became abundantly clear that everything now hinged on the ability of a political leader to build a party that could win elections, maintain control in the assembly, and so conduct an effective administration.

The first step towards stability was the final acceptance by Conservatives in Canada that features of English society could not be duplicated in the form of local hereditary elites and a local Anglican establishment. Between the 1830's and the 1850's, old-fashioned Canadian Tories learned many disagreeable lessons. In particular, they had to accept that British governments would not provide the necessary support to uphold their pretensions of privilege; they were not treated as a natural colonial ruling class. The changes in imperial economic policy during this same period as Britain moved from colonial preference to free trade were a further blow to the Tory world. By the end of the 1840's, Tory sensibilities were deeply hurt. Their encouragement of the 1849 Montreal riots was an outward manifestation of the anguish of a lost cause. In their desperation, Tories turned to some strange stratagems. Henry Boulton, for example, called for an elected legislative council in the 1850's, presumably in the hope of checking the superior strength of the Reform-influenced assembly.[4] But younger and more moderate Conservatives, like John A. Macdonald, saw the futility of further constitutional tinkering and the danger of trying to hold on to what privileges were left. Macdonald played the major role in settling the contentious church and state issues during the 1854 session. He understood much more clearly than other Conservatives that the struggle now had to be taken into the constituencies. The compact Tories' great weakness, he perceived, was that they had "no strength in numbers."[5] In the 1850's, Macdonald began changing the Conservatives from groups hoping to derive their authority from prestige to a party organized in the constituencies. Thus, by the mid-1850's, all the major constitutional issues had been settled and the old exclusive Tory ideology had been pushed to the outer fringes of the political world.

The second requirement for stability, following the English pattern, was the building of a successful party, and this was a much longer and more difficult process. Responsible government, as implemented after 1844, and more especially, as defined in practical working terms between 1848 and 1851 by Elgin, LaFontaine, and Baldwin, had removed the governor as the maker of administrations. The new cabinet-makers had to be the political leaders who could so manage the constituencies as to produce a party majority over a number of years in the legislature. This was no easy task in the Union. For a start, parties were not accustomed to discipline. Under the old system and continuing into the Union period, even members of the council with similar political views did not act in concert. As late as 1843-44, during the desperate political struggle, William Draper had great difficulty in persuading his conciliar colleagues to pull as a team.[6] Within the legislature, there were many factional and personal cross currents that made it difficult to gauge how party voting would form on particular issues. At the opening of each session, speeches were eagerly listened to in an effort to assess how various political notables were thinking on the questions of the day.[7] Within the constituencies, there would often be several party members competing for the same seat in the legislature. This was particularly true of the emerging Conservative party. Throughout the 1850's, Macdonald complained about instances where there was "a multiplicity of candidates on our side." It was essential, if the party were to become a solid institution, that as many as possible be "choked" off and the party unite behind one candidate. "We are losing everywhere from our friends splitting the party" wrote Macdonald, "if this continues it is all up with us."[8]

In these conditions and given the loosely structured nature of Canadian society, the infant parties were forced to turn to some more solidly established social institutions. The politicians looked, as we have seen, to churches and organizations such as the Orange Order to give some backbone to the amoeba-like parties. This was why Baldwin was so anxious, once in power, to attack the Orange lodges—because he regarded them as a solid base of Tory support.[9] This was why the Catholic church in Quebec, but also in Ontario, was such a major factor from this time onwards through the remainder of the century and beyond. Bishops and priests became directly involved with party leaders in fighting elections and maintaining party organization.

The powerful position of the Catholic church in Quebec was critical for any political leader who hoped to build up an effective governing party. The French-Canadian electorate, because of the church and because of the struggle, especially after the Act of Union, to protect their language and institutions, was the most salient political fact in Canada. The English-Canadian vote in the Montreal area and the small knot of rouge support among liberal bourgeois francophones in Montreal did not alter this fundamental reality. Macdonald, the clear-headed politician, saw this and understood all its ramifications. The French-Canadian electorate had to be the "sheet anchor" of a successful party. Where other Tories and Reform leaders in Canada West viewed French-Canadian support as useful on some issues but distasteful in general, a political factor that had to be dealt with in the short-run but not accommodated to in permanent structural terms, Macdonald saw that far into the future no party could gain and hold power unless it included French Canadians. As he explained to Brown Chamberlin in 1856, "no man in his senses can suppose that this country can for a century to come be governed by a totally unfrenchified government."[10]

The key to the new political game then was to build on this French-Canadian base. But political and constitutional conditions in the Union made success in this quest difficult to achieve. During the 1840's the English-Canadian Reformers in Canada West had co-operated with the French-Canadian electorate to break down the old exclusive system of government, but once this major goal was accomplished, the lack of common ground and the absence of other shared goals became apparent. The two great leaders of the coalition, LaFontaine and Baldwin, were conservative men who believed all the important tasks—the introduction of responsible government, the official recognition of the French language, the dismantling of church and seigneurial privileges—had been achieved or were well on their way to being settled. They had both retired from politics by 1851, turning their backs on the task of maintaining a permanent party organization. By the late 1840's Francis Hincks was complaining of Baldwin and LaFontaine that they did "not *lead* enough."[11] The departure of the pair with their aloof approaches to government and politics opened the way within the Reform movement for an approach more embedded in the North American rural and democratic conditions characteristic of the vast region west of Toronto.

These conditions and the vitality of local communities generated a shift away from Baldwin's whiggism to a Reform party displaying characteristic marks of genuine "country" ideology. The Grit movement, which in the 1850's and 1860's went from strength to strength in the electoral districts north and west of Toronto, was localistic and anti-statist. It wished to reduce the size of government, replace patronage-appointed officials with elected officials, and break remaining links between government, church hierarchies, and church-sponsored schools.[12] On these issues, they were at cross-purposes with the mass of the French-Canadian electorate. The gap between erstwhile allies became even wider as the population of Canada West grew and passed the population of Canada East. The Grits turned to the democratic cry of "representation by population" and charged that the system of equal representation allowed undue French-Canadian influence on politics in the Union. In their 1859 convention, the Grits codified their democratic localism into proposals for making government more responsive to the people by introducing representation by population and by applying the elective principal to as many public officials as possible.[13] Thus, after 1851, the Reform coalition broke up, and the party now rested on a Grit base with its strength in the western districts. The occasional working alliance with the small *rouge* group of lawyers and journalists in Montreal was no substitute for the mass support LaFontaine had formerly brought to the Reformers. The Grits felt proud of their democratic principles, but they had given up on the French-Canadian alliance, the essential ingredient of party success.

The increasingly cohesive moderate Conservatives forming under Macdonald in the late 1840's and early 1850's were, therefore, provided with a golden opportunity to make what Lord Elgin described as a "natural alliance" with the French-Canadian electorate.[14] The alliance was natural, believed Elgin, because English-Canadian Conservatives and the majority of French Canadians shared similar attitudes and beliefs with respect to government and society — they believed in some social hierarchy accompanied by deference to authority; they believed in appointive government and the virtues and legitimacy of patronage; they accepted the pervasive influence of venerable churches as beneficial, and they distrusted pure democracy. This new alliance of French-Canadian *bleus*, Conservatives, and some moderate Reformers from Canada West was in place by 1854 as the Conservative party. (They called themselves the Liberal-Conservative party to reflect the conservative-moderate reform combination.) In a brief and unrepeated burst of creativity they tackled the religious and constitutional issues that still caused bitter attacks on the establishment. By settling the old questions about the clergy reserves, seigneurial tenure, and state support for church colleges, Macdonald and Cartier hoped to end once and for all criticism of the political system and thus deny issues to the opposition. But although the Conservative party was able to hang onto office for nearly all the decade from 1854 to 1864, it did not succeed in building up a strong enough party to overwhelm opposition and govern effectively.

This was partly owing to the lingering problem of party discipline as ministers found they could not always count on regular attendance, far less regular support from members of the legislature. It was also related to the fixed representative structure of the Union; the Canada West wing of the party, in spite of Macdonald's efforts disparaging democratic tendencies, found it more and more difficult to resist the popular appeal of representation by population.[15] While Macdonald and Cartier were able to cling to the

French-Canadian anchor, they saw their support in Canada West become more and more shaky. Thus, because of conditions in the Union, neither the Grits nor the Conservatives were able to form effective governments. While there was nothing comparable to the turmoil of the 1828-48 period, the system remained in an unsettled state. Canada depended on British capital, but British investors saw the signs of the times, and Canadian bonds made heavy weather of it on the London markets.[16] The Union of the Canadas still suffered from political instability and was a bad bet for the future.

The obstacles to successful party development were removed by the creation of Confederation. In 1864, George Brown, the Grit leader, entered into a coalition with Macdonald and Cartier with the express purpose of solving the Union's intractable political problems by redividing the Canadas on some sort of federal basis. This Union scheme coalesced with closer union developments in the Maritime colonies and culminated in the British North American Confederation of 1867. In terms of party development, the contribution of Confederation from 1864 onwards was that it broke up the opposition Grits and provided the Conservative party with the additional strength needed to become a successful party of government.

George Brown played a critically helpful role in this respect by first of all agreeing to enter the coalition and ceasing the ideological warfare against Macdonald's party and then by pulling out of the coalition once Confederation was achieved, while leaving in place several of his most influential political colleagues. Macdonald seized this opportunity to attach this collaborative section of the opposition permanently. He distributed government patronage liberally to these former Reform colleagues and to supporters in their constituencies. When loyal Conservatives complained of valuable plums being given to former Grit opponents, Macdonald sharply retorted that as long as these men supported the Conservative party, they would receive all encouragement to stay in the fold. To a group of Conservative supporters in Toronto who complained about patronage flowing to Reform members of the government, Macdonald replied characteristically: "As soon as Toronto returns Conservative members it will get Conservative appointments, but not before."[17] Macdonald knew how to deploy executive power foresightedly in the cause of party. In addition to patronage distribution in the localities, Macdonald gave these new allies themselves important posts in the new regime. The appointment of William Macdougall as lieutenant-governor of the Northwest Territory may have been wise in terms of Macdougall's interest in the West and his alleged administrative abilities, but it also made eminent sense as part of Macdonald's strategy for building up his party.[18]

As a final psychological swipe at the Grit remnants, Macdonald insisted that now that Confederation was achieved (and since all the ancient issues of contention, such as the clergy reserves and representation by population had been settled), there were no issues to divide parties.[19] All factions should bury feelings aroused in the divisive past and unite behind the new government of the Dominion. Macdonald seems genuinely to have believed in this line of reasoning. Genuine or not, the belief provided Macdougall and his ilk with moral justification for their collaborative course and enabled Macdonald to portray his party as extending and consolidating work as part of a new-found nation-building approach to politics. Those who remained in stubborn Grit opposition were portrayed as disloyal, perhaps even treasonous. Thus, by effective patronage distribution and by exploiting the spirit of Confederation, Macdonald was successful in attaching yet another political grouping to his cause. The 1854 alliance had provided the initial base of strength; the coalition of 1864 and its continuance after 1867 pushed the Conservatives on to the commanding heights.

Macdonald's role in party-building was uniquely important during these stages. It was not that Macdonald had been born with some extra quality lacking in other political leaders but that conditions forced him to think and work harder at politics than his opponents. Throughout the Union period, the electoral trend was slowly in favour of the Reformers and then the Grit opposition in English-speaking Canada West.[20] Conservatives like Macdonald were hampered by the burden of the compact Tory past which still tinged right-wing sections of the party and still affected popular images of the party. Moreover, this tension between Tories and moderate Conservatives often made it difficult to enforce electoral and voting discipline among Conservative supporters and members of the legislature. Macdonald saw how essential it was in these conditions to attach the Canada West Conservatives to the great *bleu* strength in Canada East, but he had to contend constantly with the traditional prejudices of his English-speaking supporters. He had to manage matters so that both English and French sections of the party would remain solidly loyal to the cause. He did so by convincing his Quebec supporters that he took them seriously without giving them too much power and initiative. Macdonald, as Keith Johnson has shown, shared many of the common assumptions of Victorian Englishmen about the superiority of English culture and institutions, yet he was firmly convinced that a "frenchified" government would have to be the norm in Canada.[21] He also did it by providing a "pay-off" for those who were committed to the enlarged party, spending an immense amount of time and energy on the distribution of patronage and the other perquisites of office. These were the circumstances — the initial weakness of the Conservative party in the 1840's, the need to work with French-Canadians, the struggle to extend the base of the party — that made Macdonald work harder at politics than any of his contemporaries. And his hard work paid off in the form of an enlarged, more disciplined

Conservative party that wielded power twenty-four years out of the twenty-nine from 1867 to 1896.

The most important tool for strengthening and disciplining the party was patronage, which had been at the centre of post-1791 politics in Upper and Lower Canada. The place of patronage was re-inforced during the 1840's as Governors Metcalfe and Elgin allowed their ministers to make comprehensive use of it to improve their political position. The Reform administration under LaFontaine and Baldwin systematically distributed official posts to supporters as part of its effort to bring new social groups into the political nation and finally destroy the exclusive core of the old system. During the 1850's, Macdonald further refined the uses of patronage. He understood how patronage could be used to maximize electoral efforts, advising Ogle Gowan, judge and party activist, for example, that promises of appointments to many aspirants before an election would be much better for the party than making a smaller number of actual appointments before polling day.[22] He also tried to insist that job seekers could only approach the party through its members in the legislature and the official party organization in each district. Instead of haphazard and personalized methods of rewarding sympathizers and friends, Macdonald tried to ensure that patronage was given only in return for hard, dedicated work on behalf of the party. The trouble with the old Tory approach to patronage was that social and personal considerations had played too prominent a role. The Compact Tories, Macdonald complained to Ogle Gowan in 1847, "cannot abide promotion or employment of any one beyond their pale."[23]

By the time of Confederation, Macdonald had even formulated his constitutional justification for this now major characteristic of Canadian politics that "in the distribution of government patronage we carry out the true constitutional principle |that| whenever an office is vacant it belongs to the party supporting the government."[24] No British prime minister could have made such a statement by 1871. Even an American politician could not have committed himself to such a constitutional principle. Patronage in the United States was not justified by anything in the constitution, but it could be tolerated on the grounds that changing offices as a new party took power was democracy at work.[25] Only in Canada was partisan patronage distribution given a constitutional legitimacy. As Goldwin Smith archly remarked in 1883, Macdonald proclaimed "as the verdict of his personal experience, that Acts of Parliament can be satisfactorily carried into effect only by the Friends of Government, an avowal of the Spoils System which would startle by its frankness, even if it came from the lips of an American politician."[26]

Macdonald spent an extraordinary amount of time on the details of patronage. Right down until his final election, he collected and scrutinized information that helped him strengthen the party. As he conceded during the Pacific Scandal of 1873, he spent much more time on party management than would a contemporary British prime minister. He explained to Dufferin that had he been in office in England, he "should have left it to our Carlton and Reform Clubs."[27] In an earlier note to Carnarvon, the prime minister had urged the Colonial Secretary to appreciate that in a "new country" like Canada "public men are much harder worked and are obliged to attend to more details than they are in England."[28] As late in his life and career as the winter of 1888-89, he was analysing the composition of the bar in Toronto and throughout Ontario to identify which lawyers were for him and which ones supported "the enemy."[29]

From the moment he assumed leadership of the Tory-Conservative cause in the early-1850's until his death in 1891, Macdonald was on a political treadmill, spending his time not simply on policies but also on the effective deployment of patronage. As Keith Johnson has perceptively observed, this was a treadmill of Macdonald's own making and Macdonald certainly enjoyed all the details (at least, after the 1850's when his system began to be successful). He came to life in politics.[30] He did not use patronage for personal, selfish, or temporary ends (as he believed the Compact Tories had done). Indeed, Macdonald's great impact was owing to the fact that he made a continuing effort to ensure that patronage was used to build up permanent party loyalty and resilient party discipline. He had little sympathy for friends such as Alexander Campbell, a Tory holdover who wished rewards without putting in the necessary quota of party work during successive elections. When it was time to fight elections, Campbell remained distant and patronizing. Macdonald and Campbell, explained Joseph Pope, were "never kindred spirits . . . for Campbell remained a Tory aristocrat . . . when elections were to be fought, Campbell if he did not find he had business elsewhere, was disposed to look on in a patronizing sort of way. He seldom took off his coat or even his gloves in the fight but he always turned up when the victory was won. Sir John resented this."[31] He insisted that all applicants have a lengthy, demonstrable record of party service. Writing in 1883, J.E. Collins was struck by the marked changes in the Conservative party of the 1840's under Macdonald's methods. "It would," noted Collins, "give much scandal to the Conservative of this day who prizes loyalty to his party as not among the least of the political virtues to walk back forty years into the ages and from the gallery of the Canadian assembly see the discord and disunity in the Conservative party then."[32]

In an important way, Macdonald's personal supervision of and deep interest in the whole range of government patronage was a necessary ingredient for success. Otherwise, it might have had a divisive and fragmenting impact with other notables and factions within the party fighting to seize it for their own ends. An ironical treatise written in 1832 by Henry Taylor, an

English civil servant, bears an unintended relevance to Macdonald in this regard. Taylor argued that it would be best to keep control of patronage in as few hands as possible to ensure that it was used in the public interest. The "minister who has been long in office will be the most likely to dispense his patronage properly, for the circle of private friends is saturated."[33] Thus, because he steered patronage towards the single purpose of party-building and because he stayed in power so long, Macdonald was able to use this technique effectively. Those who were outside Macdonald's system or who took a high moral line on these aspects of Canadian politics were sometimes outraged. In 1891, Daniel Wilson, president of the University of Toronto, upon news of Macdonald's death, derided the eulogists who called Macdonald "a great statesman." Macdonald, fumed Wilson (while still unable to shake off his admiration for the man), was "a clever, most unprincipled party leader [who] had developed a system of political corruption that has demoralised the country. Its evils will long survive him . . . nevertheless he had undoubtedly a fascinating power of conciliation, which, superadded to his unscrupulous use of patronage, and systematic bribery in every form, has enabled him to play off province against province and hold his own against every enemy but the invincible last antagonist."[34]

Goldwin Smith, in an uncharacteristic moment of fairness to Macdonald, saw even deeper into the significance of Macdonald's success. The Conservative party, he wrote in 1883, was now bound together "by an artificer who, in the course of a long career has acquired a thorough knowledge of all the men, the interests and the passions with which he has to deal, uses that knowledge with considerable skill and shrinks from the employment of no means of influence, while, like Walpole, in the midst of corruption, he remains personally pure."[35] Smith sensed and appreciated the parallel between Walpole and Macdonald. Both men had worked extremely hard at the details to create stable parties of government after long years of political turmoil.

Macdonald's vision on the nature and consequences of his approach to politics was perfectly clear. A telling example was his definition of "the long game" success formula in the new Canadian politics. Macdonald made this remark in the midst of a discussion of the performance of John Sandfield Macdonald as Ontario premier (1867-71) and leader of the Liberal Conservatives in Ontario. Macdonald was critical of Sandfield Macdonald for not exploiting office effectively. The Ontario premier had conducted a "thrifty . . . penurious administration of affairs" when he should have created more departments and hence increased his stock of public appointments. There was revenue available for this but, lamented Macdonald, he "did not have the pluck to use [it]." Macdonald had pressed his Ontario counterpart "to make a President of the Council and a Minister of Education [and] with those two offices and that of Solicitor-General and the Speakership he had the game in his own hands." Macdonald had also urged Sandfield Macdonald to hold on to power until the federal Conservatives had won the upcoming elections and returned to power. "Once in possession of the reins for the next five years," he explained, "we can bring tremendous leverage to help you in the Local Legislature in the session 1872-73." Then Macdonald added, "depend upon it, the long game is the true one." Macdonald's "long game," therefore, had nothing to do with his policy initiatives. It was the game of political patronage and influence to strengthen party, a game he had worked on since the 1840's, a game that the Sandfield Macdonalds and George Browns of the world were too timid and too restricted in their political vision to play.[36] They certainly did not play it with Macdonald's foresighted and comprehensive thoroughness.

An even more explicit confirmation of Macdonald's priorities came in 1885, following the passage of the Franchise Act. In the course of planning, passing, and implementing the legislation, Macdonald accumulated volumes of detail about county judges and barristers throughout the country, but especially in Ontario, as part of his effort to make sure the new revising officers would not weaken the Conservative cause. It was a veritable *tour de force* in patronage deployment, for while taking great pains to appoint the right type of judge or barrister as revising officer from the Conservative party standpoint, Macdonald was able to claim he was exercising legitimate executive powers.[37] He was able to obscure his course because of "the Constitutional drapery transmitted from a previous state of things in which the sovereign power was the Crown."[38] The opposition was outraged by this successful attempt at comprehensive electoral influence. The debates on the legislation were the longest and most bitter since Confederation had been established.[39] But the Conservative party was now loyal and disciplined, and the bill became law. Macdonald called this "the greatest triumph of my life."[40]

That has been an odd assessment for modern scholars to understand. Macdonald's role in settling the church establishment questions of the 1850's, his role in bringing about Confederation, his efforts on behalf of the Canadian Pacific Railway, and his formulation of the "national policy" after 1878 have outranked the achievement of the Franchise Act in the view of historians. But not for Macdonald himself. As he looked at his political career—the disunity and weakness of the 1840's, the tiring efforts at party building in the 1850's, the need to join a coalition in 1864, and the collapse in 1873 because of the wretched Pacific Scandal—the position of the party by the mid-1880's seemed exceptionally solid. In the franchise business, as in so much else, he had done most of the work himself. If modern scholars have had some difficulty in appreciating the "greatest triumph" remark, Governors Sydenham and Metcalfe would have understood.[41] They too had tried to do everything themselves from setting policy priorities to influencing elections. They had failed. Macdonald had triumphed. In his remark, Macdonald revealed how much his outlook on politics had congealed in the 1840's.[42] More than any other single figure, Macdonald played a central role in moulding Canadian political culture. His success and longevity gave traditional attitudes towards politics and patronage an extended lease on life for decades beyond Confederation.

The centrality of patronage in Canadian political culture was, then, confirmed and entrenched by the way in which responsible government had come about in the 1840's and by Macdonald's long dominance from 1854 to 1891. He believed the powers formerly exercised by governors should be exercised by the political leaders who were chosen, and who were strong enough, to run the administration. This is why he believed patronage and influence were entirely legitimate tools in the Canadian setting. And this is what made him extremely powerful by the 1880's as a prime minister; he was unchecked by Crown or peers or other established centres of power. As J.C. Dent perceptively observed, Macdonald had "won his way to more than vice-regal power."[43] Thus, at the very moment when patronage was disappearing as a factor that cemented parties in England,[44] it became a characteristic feature of Canadian party development. Lord Dufferin, although phrasing the point in a condescending manner, had insight into this divergence of Canadian from the mid Victorian British pattern when he remarked that Macdonald was "certainly the best statesman in Canada though too prone to maintain his power by expedients condemned by the higher moral standard of modern politics."[45]

So successful was Macdonald's approach, so natural it seemed in the context of Canadian developments since 1791, that his opponents gradually adopted his methods in the decades after Confederation. Back in 1859, the Grits had hoped to shift party government on to a more democratic path with smaller government and much greater elective control of public officials. George Brown had cleaved to these classical liberal positions, and the Liberal party under the leadership of Alexander Mackenzie (and under the pressure of economic recession) stopped short of the comprehensive Macdonaldian use of patronage. Like all administrations since the 1840's, Mackenzie's Liberal government between 1874 and 1878 did fill posts through patronage, but the prime minister had genuine misgivings on this score. Mackenzie was "sickened" by letters from supporters containing "just the sort of requests for partisan favours that he had criticised for so many years."[46] Mackenzie's successor as Liberal party leader had too intellectual an approach to politics to adopt Macdonald's methods. Edward Blake, Liberal party leader from 1880 to 1887, "found politics dishonest and corrupt."[47]

Mackenzie and Blake were also out of sympathy with another, related aspect of Macdonald's approach to politics. The growth of government was an important underpinning of the Macdonald system, but because of contemporary economic conditions and also because of the traditional liberal view, Mackenzie sought to cut back and restrict government's reach in society and the economy.[48]

The first change in Liberal attitudes occurred not at the federal level but among the Ontario Liberals under the leadership of Oliver Mowat, premier of Ontario from 1872 to 1896.[49] Macdonald saw the early warning signs. When Mowat took over the premiership, Macdonald noted that "as I prophesied would be the case, the first act of the new Government was to increase the Cabinet."[50] Throughout the 1870's and 1880's, Mowat built up the Ontario Liberal party by the same methods as Macdonald had used in building up the federal Conservatives. This was one of the reasons they fought so hard over respective government spheres—each needed to expand the administration he controlled as much as possible to strengthen his respective party.[51] The dynamics of this process at the local level can be seen clearly in a long letter sent to their federal MPs by Conservative party notables in Lindsay, Ontario. This petition, sent through Hector Cameron and Arthur McQuade, the two sitting members, was designed to explain how the future of party battles was related to patronage. The Lindsay Conservatives, first of all, asked that a junior judgeship be created in Victoria county. The appointment of a judge sympathetic to the Conservatives would enable the local Tories to defeat the incumbent Liberal member of the Ontario legislature. They argued that "owing to the influence and patronage in the hands of the Stipendary Magistrate of Haliburton, the Local Member for N. Victoria will continue to be Reform as long as that officer continues in a position to use his influence and patronage but if a Junior Judge be appointed here the people of that County will unite in asking that their Division Courts be held by the Judge of Victoria and this will lessen the influence above referred to and, we trust, aid us in regaining the representation in the Local House which we always held until Mr. Peck, the former Stipendary Magistrate, was elected in 1879." This piece of patronage, in short, would help defeat the Mowat Reformer who was an important source of Liberal strength in the area.

To improve their case, the Lindsay Conservatives pointed out to Macdonald that Mowat was making effective use of patronage to strengthen the local Liberals and implied that Macdonald would need to give more patronage to keep up local Conservatives' strength and morale. The local party had kept track of all patronage appointments since 1861, and they enclosed a list of these:

Statement of Appointments Since 1861

By Reform Government	*By Conservative Government*
1862 Judge (dead)	Collector of Customs
Sheriff (dead)	Landing Waiter
Clerk Co:Court	Official Assignees
Co:Attorney	
Clerk of Peace	
Registrar still in office	
Since Confederation	
	Judge
	Inspector of Weights and Measures
	Official Assignee
	Post-Master at Lindsay

By Local House Since Confederation
    Sheriff
    Co:Attorney
    Clerk of Peace
    License Inspector
          South Riding
    License Inspector
          North Riding
    Police Magistrate
    Issuer of Marriage Licenses
Haliburton
    Stipendary Magistrate
               (MPP, 1879)
    License Inspector

The Lindsay Conservatives were becoming alarmed at this build-up by Mowat of Reform/Liberal influence. They needed more patronage (starting with the judgeship) for future strength of their local Conservative organization.[52]

As long as the fastidious Edward Blake, with his intellectualized approach to politics, was leader of the federal Liberals, these lessons did not sink in at the national level.[53] But Wilfrid Laurier, taking over in 1887 and battling his way on an apparently unpromising course, saw the signs of the times. He came to appreciate how Macdonald and Mowat worked. The isolated core of Liberal strength in Quebec—the middle-class *rouge* party in Montreal—had been attracted to small government, even republican forms of government in the 1860's. Raoul Dandurand, subsequently a Laurier stalwart in Quebec, recalls his family dining-room in the 1860's having a lithograph of Abraham Lincoln in a place of honour. By 1900, Dandurand was nicely ensconced in his appointive Senate seat, rewarded with this patronage plum for his long years of service to the party.[54] Not the least of Laurier's achievements then was to shift the federal Liberal party to duplicate the Macdonald formula for party building. Once in office, as in so many other ways, he followed Macdonald's line on patronage. He himself paid attention to details — even down to the appointment of station-masters and porters and the hiring of temporary Christmas personnel at the post office. He tried to make sure that only dedicated party workers received posts in the public services.[55]

The rigorous application of this principle can be seen from a case in London, Ontario, in the Spring of 1900. John A. Donegan had volunteered to fight in the Boer War. He had been killed, leaving a widow and two sons to fend for themselves. Family friends approached the government for posts in the public service. It might be expected that in this part of Ontario, in the midst of the war, such a family might have received sympathetic treatment from the Liberal party. But this was not to be so, for the crucial element was missing — the Donegans had not been active workers for the party. As George Reid, the local leader of the Liberal organization, reminded Laurier, it would be very unpopular to make a position for either of the Donegans in the locality. "They have never been friends of ours in any particular and it would never do to appoint any one who has not been identified with the work of the party. . . . To appoint him for any position simply because his Father was killed in Africa would be to my mind very absurd."[56] This was the authentic voice of the Laurier Liberals on patronage matters. In power between 1896 and 1911, the party deployed patronage for the same purposes and in the same manner as the Conservatives between 1867 and 1896. They expanded government; they even had in the Canadian Northern Railway an equivalent source of jobs and contracts that Macdonald had had with the Grand Trunk and the Canadian Pacific.[57]

Thus, throughout the entire post-Confederation period from 1867 to 1910, both national parties used patronage as the cement of party. In itself, of course, it was not sufficient. The party leaders had to deal with policy issues, with regional and factional tensions, and with the whole array of day-to-day matters that came within the purview of a prime minister and his cabinet. All that may be granted; yet the fact remains that patronage was a preoccupation of the party leaders. This was a distinguishing characteristic of Canadian political culture. Patronage was the ballast which enabled the political ship to make headway. In 1904, Lord Minto, with his outsider's perspective, saw this hallmark of Canadian politics. The people of Canada, he forecast, "must eventually decide whether their public appointments are to be administered for their own good or for the benefit of a political party."[58]

When he made that assertion about public appointments being used exclusively for partisan purposes, Minto may well have been jaundiced by his failure to get his own way on the militia question. But he was perfectly accurate in assessment of how things worked in Canada. Thoughtful and well-informed Canadians, both at Minto's time and since, have confirmed its validity. Comprehensive investigations of the public service were conducted in 1868-69, 1880-81, 1891-92, 1907-08 and 1911-12 and provided ample evidence that the party in power had no hesitation in linking all public appointments to party goals.[59] Some of the most renowned modern historians of Canada have concurred in this judgment. Patronage, W. L. Morton has written, was "the natural currency of political life," and the power to distribute patronage was what gave cabinet office its "meaning and substance."[60] In the same vein, Peter B. Waite, in his authoritative account of the 1874-96 years, has remarked that during his long tenure as minister of customs, Mackenzie Bowell's "principal preoccupation was patronage."[61] There is then abundant contemporary evidence and later scholarly confirmation that patronage, which had been of prime importance to the Tory elites under the 1791 constitution and which was at the centre of the political warfare of the 1840's had become in the 1867-1910 period the major binding material for political parties.

The scale and penetration of patronage must be fully appreciated to understand its impact. In 1877, a parliamentary select committee to inquire into "the present condition of the Civil Service" concluded that "the exercise of political patronage seems to be almost unchecked." The public service of the dominion was not viewed as "an organisation for conducting the public business |but| as a means of rewarding personal and political friends."[62] In 1908, thirty years later and after nineteen years of Conservative and ten of Liberal government, the Civil Service Commission saw no change in Canadian conditions. The commissioners reported bluntly that "patronage seems to run more or less through every department of the public service." Far from seeing any signs that patronage was diminishing as Canada entered the twentieth century, on the basis of the evidence they had uncovered, the commissioners concluded that patronage was stronger than ever. "The public service," they wrote, "not only at Ottawa but elsewhere throughout the Dominion, has fallen back during the last fifteen years."[63] On paper, the party in power was limited in its ability to exploit the public service in this manner, but throughout these years the Civil Service Act (1868) was ignored or circumvented. "Act after Act," R. Macgregor Dawson showed, "has been passed, some whittling away a few appointments under an existing statute, others taking from the Civil Service Commission control of whole groups of public servants, others setting up new positions and exempting them from the operation of the Civil Service Act."[64] The contemporary reforms in the British public service after 1869 had little impact on Canada where the traditional practice of regarding the civil service "mainly as a means of rewarding court or party favourites persisted well into the twentieth century."[65]

The 1907-08 commissioners made a comprehensive and detailed indictment of the system. There had been, ever since 1882, a Board of Civil Service Examiners, but it had minimal impact on reducing political patronage. Two members of the board (both having served since its inception) explained that both federal parties had routinely by-passed or undermined the examination structure. The most usual technique was simply to classify groups of officers in ways "not laid down in the Civil Service Act." There had been, in fact, "a constant attempt to evade the examinations." The commissioners were struck by the systematic manner in which both Conservative and Liberal administrations had pursued their patronage courses. In one department alone in Ottawa (Department of the Interior), 350 employees had been classified in a way which excluded them from the terms of the Civil Service Act, and "a very great number are also outside the provision of the Act in the Departments of Agriculture, Marine and Fisheries, Public Works and Railways and Canals."

Outside of Ottawa it was even more common for public officials not to be regulated by the act. The commissioners reported that "no Dominion Lands Agent, no Indian Agent, no officer of the Intercolonial Railway, no outside officer of the Public Works Department is under the provisions of the Act and members of the Northwest Mounted Police, together with many other sets of officials, are excluded from its provisions." The commissioners became convinced as they examined all this evidence that "as a rule in the outside service . . . politics enter into every appointment and politicians on the spot interest themselves not only in the appointments but in the subsequent promotion of officers." In a phrase replicating Minto's view, the commissioners concluded that "in the outside service the politics of the party is of greater importance in making appointments and promotions than the public interests of the Dominion."[66]

Particular investigations of individual departments confirmed these general assessments. In the case of the Customs Department, "every collector of customs has been appointed from the ranks of the party in power at the moment." Although the outside service of the customs department was supposed to be covered by the Civil Service Act, a clause in that act waiving the examination for posts that required technical expertise was invoked to avoid coverage by the act. For example, in Winnipeg "no officer in the service has ever passed an examination."[67] A detailed investigation (by Judge C.T. Cassells) of the Department of Marine and Fisheries revealed a similar pattern. Jobs and contracts were invariably given to party supporters recommended by the local MP. "The system," noted Cassells, "seems to have been handed down from administration to administration since Confederation . . . It is apparently based on the old maxim 'to the victor belong the spoils,' utterly ignoring the fact that the money to be disbursed is mainly contributed by the people generally and not the money of the political followers of the party at that time being in power."[68] The civil service commissioners in 1908, therefore, believed that the system had "few redeeming features" and that it was a deeply embedded characteristic of Canadian political life. "The trouble," they observed, "is not of recent origin but has long continued and is the result of evil methods and practices prescribed for many years."[69]

These investigations of 1877 and 1907-08 delineate with abundant supporting evidence the unrelenting nature of Canadian political patronage—like water finding its own level, it penetrated to all areas of society and the economy that came within purview of the Ottawa government. The omnipresence of patronage is perhaps most tellingly revealed in the legal profession because this was one sphere, especially in the appointment of judges, where Macdonald was believed to put aside party considerations and act in a high-minded fashion.[70] Yet when he considered each new batch of Queen's Counsel (QC) nominations, Macdonald only looked favourably on those lawyers who had a record of work on behalf of the Conservative party. The criteria that counted with the prime minister were nicely set out in some 1887 correspondence between Macdonald and John Small.[71] In a confidential memorandum, Small listed those lawyers eligible for QC. He noted against each name when the man had been admitted to the bar (a standing of twelve years at the bar was required) and the firm for which the nominee worked. Small then completed his list with the following essential information:

Michael Murphy—defeated candidate 1882 . . . attended meetings in recent elections . . . Roman Catholic.
Daniel DeFoe—a strong supporter, always took a prominent part in political movements.
James Reeve—did good work at the last election.
James Fullerton—takes the platform in the interests of the party.
George Blackstock—has contested elections.
Emerson Coatsworth—rising young barrister, pillar of the Methodist Church, a strong Temperance advocate, President of the Liberal-Conservative Association for his Ward, was my agent in last election.

All of these candidates for QC had a variety of characteristics. Their role in churches was obviously an important consideration, another sign of the close links between organized religion and the political parties that had been present since the 1840's. Yet, in spite of the variety of church affiliation, all shared one necessary qualification. They were all active party workers, not simply supporters, but men who contributed time and effort to the cause—

they were, to use a phrase of the day, "cold water" men prepared to work for the party "in season and out."[72] Without this, they could not hope to be considered. It was well-nigh impossible to get ahead in the legal profession unless you were so identified with a party. To belong to neither party was to be morally suspect as a lawyer without principles—political ballast was essential for steering the conventional legal career. A man without party was derided as a "weathercock," waiting to shift course according to the party fortunes of the day. Such a man was considered to be pursuing his own selfish career goals—"an unscrupulous professional man."[73] The matter-of-fact recognition of this intimate linkage between lawyers and party-building in post-Confederation Canada can be seen in a letter to Macdonald from Robert Birmingham, a leading organizer in the Conservative Union of Ontario. In October 1889, Birmingham sent Macdonald "the names of a few Legal Friends who have rendered us special service in the recent campaign in the hope you might be able to repay them with the much sought after QC."[74]

Beyond the bar was the bench. And as with all other public appointments, judgeships went only to those who had served the party in power. Indeed, since judgeships were so important in terms of social status and political influence, anyone who hoped to become a judge had to have a very substantial and demonstrable track record of partisan work. This does not mean that Macdonald does not deserve some of the high reputation with respect to judgeships which his secretary and biographer Joseph Pope laboured to bestow upon him. There were usually enough aspirants for a judgeship that Macdonald could choose someone with strong legal credentials, but as with QCs, no one could enter the competition without the record of party work.

The way in which judgeships were handed out is well illustrated in an 1879 case from Oxford county, Ontario. In this instance, Alexander Finkle of Woodstock mounted a campaign for the junior judgeship of the county. In a letter to the prime minister, Finkle explained that "as Junior Judge I would be acceptable to the leading Conservatives in this county."[75] This essential qualification was confirmed by local party notables in letters on behalf of Finkle. The President of the Conservative association of the North Riding of Oxford wrote of Finkle that "his claims on the party stand as high as any gentleman in the county." Macdonald was also warned by these local party leaders against a rival aspirant for the judgeship. This rival (K.B. Beard) was "looked upon as an unscrupulous professional man and in politics carries two faces under one head." Beard was painted as a career-minded lawyer, seeking his own way, and certainly not a tried and true Conservative. To make judges of men like Beard would demoralize the local party. Finkle was the right type. In contrast to Beard, he had "always been a steadfast Conservative."[76] J.W. Nesbitt, from Holbrook, added his endorsement, telling Macdonald that Finkle's appointment "would be appreciated by your friends here as he has always been a *staunch* Conservative."[77] The refrain continued in a note from A. McCloughlin of Woodstock, who praised Finkle as "a sound lawyer and a true party man." He has, continued the argument, "ever been a constant supporter of your government and any advantage that may befall him through the efforts of political friends will be but a just recognition of past services."[78] Summing up Finkle's case from London, John Carling wrote to Macdonald, "I do not think that you could appoint a better man or one who has worked harder in the interests of the party."[79] Finkle, "the true party man," received his judgeship.[80]

It was never enough for an aspiring lawyer to be an occasional contributor to party funds or to turn out only in the midst of an election campaign. Long years of hard work in good times and bad on behalf of the party was the prerequisite. This was amply demonstrated in another of Macdonald's appointments to the bench, this time a county judgeship in Hastings. The local Conservative notables campaigned for E.B. Fraleck. W.L. Payne, a Conservative lawyer, noted that Fraleck had

> always been most active in the Conservative party not only in the ridings in the County of Hastings but also in East Northumberland and has spared neither time nor money in completing the organization of the party. [His appointment as county judge] would be well received by the party and would be taken as a recognition of faithful services."[81]

The president of the Conservative Association of West Hastings added his weight, reminding Macdonald that Fraleck was "a staunch supporter of the Conservative cause and a very hard worker at all the Elections and very successful also. We therefore think him well qualifide [sic] to fill the possition [sic] of Judge."[82] Alexander Robertson of Belleville, for whom Fraleck had worked in election campaigns, sounded the familiar theme. Fraleck

> has been more useful by his energy and industry on the occasion of Elections than any other member of the Conservative party. The reaction in Sidney, which is strongly Grit, at my first Election when we carried the Township by nine majority is in great measure attributable to the time spent with me in the Township by Mr. Fraleck. I think this appointment would give our friends here great satisfaction."[83]

All this evidence made a compelling case; Fraleck was just the sort of energetic party worker over a long number of years who ought to be rewarded "pour encourager les autres." Fraleck was appointed county judge.[84]

One final case will serve to drive home the point that political patronage was the central fact behind the appointing of judges as it was to all other sections of the public service. In this example, a party activist, B.L. Doyle, who was a lawyer, a Catholic, and a Conservative, pressed his claims for a county judgeship. He began by setting out his qualifications in a letter to Senator Frank Smith, the most influential Ontario Catholic in the upper ranks of the Conservative party. Doyle approached Smith because the latter was "familiar with my career as a Conservative for many years past and for the further fact that the prominent position you so justly hold in the Estimation of the Catholic Body of Ontario entitles you to much consideration at the hands of the Government." This appeal to Smith was made partly because Doyle knew that his Catholicism might count against him among party workers in Ontario who believed Macdonald was too solicitous of the Catholic fact in politics. Doyle then proceeded to detail his credentials for the bench, resting them on the typical basis that "my services to the Party for the past 15 years entitled me to something." He then recounted the high points of that work:

> As Sir John has just so well said of his Ottawa friends I have not simply been a "Fairweather Friend." I stood by the party in the darkest hours of its severest trials; I fought for it when it was down and persevered in the desperate struggle on behalf of our principles till the victory again crowned our efforts [the 1878 election]. Now all this you know—you met me on several occasions when I was fighting for the cause and you know whether or not I have been true. It is conceded by those who know best that in South Bruce and North Huron my efforts contributed very materially (not to claim too much) in defeating the Hon. Edward Blake and in electing Mr. Shaw and Mr. Farrow. Mr. Farrow of North Huron, an Orangeman who was elected 3 times in succession will acknowledge that without my assistance it is very doubtful, to say the least, if he would have been elected—he certainly would not at the last Election—while with my opposition he *never* could have been elected."

Doyle even claimed that he had stalwartly resisted offers from the Liberals "to silence me" by the offer of place to dramatize his devotion to the Conservative cause. Doyle believed "Sir John to be well disposed towards the Catholic body and that all he wants is the opportunity to do us justice. In my case the opportunity is at hand, and I take the liberty of asking you for the reasons I have mentioned to press my claims on the Government." Lest Senator Smith be too obtuse to grasp the point, Doyle concluded bluntly: "I want a county judgeship."[85]

This forthright, if immodest, letter had all the right ingredients to command attention. In passing on the letter to Macdonald, Senator Smith noted that Doyle's case was "worth considering as it is true, and he certainly deserves well of the Conservative party." Smith did reassure Macdonald on Doyle's legal ability ("he was a clever, intelligent and a good lawyer"), but he concentrated on the main point that Doyle was "a plucky, active man whom I know to have worked hard for his party." Smith was as blunt to Macdonald as Doyle had been to him. Doyle, wrote Smith, "deserves to get what he asks."[86] Letters were also received by Macdonald from the bishop of London and the bishop of Hamilton, the latter worthy explaining to the prime minister that Doyle had been "a strong and consistent Conservative for many years . . . . From what I know of that county, I think his appointment would go very far to unite the Catholic and Conservative vote."[87] Parish priests chipped in with notes to the effect that Doyle was "a firm supporter of your interests" and "an old supporter of the Conservative party "[88]

Macdonald found this case to be somewhat complicated in spite of (or, rather, because of) Doyle's heavy support from Smith and the Catholic hierarchy of Ontario. Some local Conservative leaders in South Bruce and North Huron, while keen to accept Doyle's electoral help, believed the appointment of a Catholic judge might cause disquiet with "our Orange friends." They put up their own candidate and urged Macdonald, if he must appoint Doyle, to look for another county.[89] Macdonald hesitated. But Doyle's case was compelling; his was the kind of loyal, dedicated work Macdonald wanted from supporters. Doyle's reward was delayed, but in the end he got it, being appointed in 1883 as junior judge in Huron.[90]

Judges and QCs were important to Macdonald, the party leader, because such men were local pillars of the community across Canada. The careful cultivation of patronage in this field was, as the foregoing evidence suggests, of great consequence to the strength and morale of the local Conservative organizations who fought the elections. There was also a more specific consideration at work. Judges and QCs were deeply involved in the validating of voters' lists and, in the early stages, in making determinations on disputed elections. This was uniformly the case after the passage of the 1885 Franchise Act when county judges or revising barristers, appointed by Ottawa, were made responsible for the validity of voters' lists. Thus, paying attention to judges and QCs was part of that tradition of executive electoral manipulation that went back to the British governors of the 1830's and 1840's. As Norman Ward, the modern authority on this topic, has shown, "the whole representative system, from periodic adjustments of constituency boundaries to post-election trials for corruption at the polls, was provided for in terms which gave Parliament wide discretion to alter it at will. For all practical purposes, the electoral machinery was thus placed in the hands of the government to be the subject of any legislation that might be

expedient . . . there was no legal or constitutional barrier to hinder manipulation."[91] As prime minister, Macdonald was "intent on converting the
electoral system into both a pool of patronage and an instrument for winning
elections."[92] The 1882 gerrymander was a fine example of this approach,
with little effort being made to conceal the partisan purposes of the legislation.
The "guiding motive of the Act was to help maintain the Conservative party
vote in Ontario."[93] So too was the guiding motive of the 1885 franchise
legislation to shore up the Conservative party position in federal elections. It
was indeed Macdonald's grand demonstration of his talents at electoral
influencing and patronage distribution in the interests of party.[94]

As we have seen, patronage and influence had become normal, pervasive,
and legitimate in Canadian political culture because of the way in which the
1791 system worked and the way in which responsible government had come
about in the Canadas. The premiers of the Union and the prime ministers
after Confederation were able to take over the powers of the governors, as
well as exercise the power due to their political weight and claim that
Canada's monarchical constitution validated their comprehensive exploita-
tion of the public service and manipulation of the electoral system.

But the system of patronage also worked so well for party leaders because
of the favourable economic and social conditions in nineteenth-century
Canada. One important condition for the successful operation of the patronage system was the fact that government was expanding throughout this
entire period when the economy as a whole experienced only uneven
growth.[95] The growth of government was sustained by three factors—the
need to overcome Canada's difficult geographical setting, which meant
large-scale government involvement in railways and canals; the need to
incorporate the new western territories; the need to build up the other
infrastructures of Confederation by the expansion of new federal departments,
by establishing post offices, customs houses, court systems, as well as all the
associated bureaucracies. That Macdonald understood the significance of
all this is clear enough at the time; for example, when he urged Sandfield
Macdonald to expand the Ontario government. The bitter struggle between
Mowat and Macdonald over such issues as liquor licensing and control of
inland waterways was largely because both party leaders understood how
beneficial government expansion was to their efforts at party consolidation.

The broader economic context after 1867 intensified the significance of
this reality. From the 1850's up to 1900, Canada did not have a dynamically
expanding capitalist economy characteristic of the United States in the
nineteenth century.[96] In an economy such as Canada's, there were only
limited opportunities for profit and for jobs. Some care must be exercised
when making generalizations about Canadian economic growth during this
period. The old view that painted a picture of painfully slow industrialization

accompanied by a population drain to the more successful American economy is much too simplistic. In this vein scholars pointed out with apparent finality that manufacturing remained on a very small scale with the average number of people employed in each industrial establishment rising from only 4.6 in 1870 to 5.5 in 1890. Supporting evidence could also be drawn from the census which in 1881 classified 81 per cent of the population as rural, and as late as 1911 showed that 76 per cent of Canadians were still living in rural areas or in towns of less than 30,000.[97] But such figures taken without elaboration are misleading. This old view of Canadian economic performance in fact tended simply to reflect the contemporary Liberal critique (subsequently endorsed by a generation of liberal historians) that Macdonald's national policy after 1878 was politically successful but economically ineffective. Recent scholarship has taken a more positive and nuanced view of Canada's post-Confederation economic performance. Peter B. Waite's fair-minded assessment in *Arduous Destiny. Canada 1874-96* draws attention to the increase in GNP for these years. While growth in the industrial sector was not spectacular, it was continuous, and although the average size of manufactories may have remained small until the end of the century, large factories dominated production in a broad range of goods in the major towns of central Canada from Montreal to Toronto, Hamilton, and London.[98]

Much recent work by Canadian historians has focused attention on this urban-industrial environment, a natural development given that it became the most common environment in which Canadians now live, but there is a real question of how quickly and how deeply these trends at the advancing edge of the economy had an impact on the political world still controlled by a generation that had grown up in an agricultural, small-town setting. The Senate Select Committee report of 1911 on "the unsatisfactory movement of population" is an example of this traditional mentality, which still hoped and expected that the new urban development would not push aside the familiar social landmarks. Politicians as intelligent and knowing as Laurier were ill at ease when it came to dealing with the demands of this new urban-industrial phenomenon.[99] Up to the end of his life Macdonald paid close attention to the prospects for each year's harvest. For many well-informed contemporaries of Macdonald and Laurier, agriculture in all its associated social and economic ramifications remained the bedrock of the economy. In 1896, in the *Monetary Times*, Byron Walker reminded Canadians that agriculture was "the substratum of our well-being." In 1898, in a speech before the Canadian Bankers Association, D.R. Wilkie told his audience that Canada "was essentially an agricultural country," and in 1907 an article in *Industrial Canada* reaffirmed that agriculture was "the very foundation of our social economy".[100]

Wherever one chooses to give emphasis in assessing Canada's economy for this period, it remains undeniable that, compared to conditions in Britain or the United States, what business activity took place was intertwined to an extraordinary degree with governments at both the federal and provincial levels. And so the business world was intimately linked with the world of political patronage. In his seminal *The Politics of Development*, which deals with the Ontario case, H.V. Nelles has shown how "business could not get along without the active co-operation of the state." In the Canadian context, businessmen turned as a matter of course to provincial and federal governments for contracts, favours, and special arrangements for particular industries. In the Ontario case, for example, there was some difficulty in attracting American investors to timber because the Americans were puzzled and distrustful of the government's policy of leasing rather than selling timber lands. This kind of state supervision was odd to American eyes.[101] In his *The Politics of Federalism*, Christopher Armstrong has demonstrated convincingly that private interests turned to one or other level of government for assistance and frequently played one off against the other.[102] While such interconnection between government and business is common enough in advanced capitalist societies, it came much earlier and more pervasively in Canada. From the Welland Canal Company in the 1820's to the feverish canal and railway building of the Union period to the great post-Confederation transportation projects, Canadian administrations had been deeply involved in managing and manipulating (and in turn being managed and manipulated by) business interests. Professor Nelles views all this as in some way a betrayal of responsible government because it shifted so much power to the administration from the democracy, and he writes of the "failure of parties and politicians to pursue the logic of responsible government into the industrial age."[103] But a counter case can be made, as this study has argued, that such a development was entirely in keeping with the Canadian "court" or statist version of responsible government. It was an unquestioned Canadian tradition that reached back to colonial times.

It was these material conditions of the Canadian economy and society that provided fruitful ground in which patronage could flourish into luxuriant growth as businessmen turned to federal and provincial governments for concessions, arrangements, jobs, and contracts. Moreover, the single biggest enterprise was government itself. The federal and provincial governments were energizing forces which took leading roles in stimulating economic growth. The nation-building enterprises at the federal level were replicated by provincial governments basing their activities on the ownership of lands, forests, and minerals.[104] The governments were also busy constructing their own physical presence in hundreds of public works projects across the new country in the form of harbours, bridges, post offices, customs houses, and other buildings to accommodate the party supporters Macdonald thought so constitutionally deserving of office in the public service. In neither Britain nor the United States did government have such reach into society and economy.

Given the uncertainties in the Canadian economy and bearing in mind Canada's modest rate of growth compared to the dramatic expansion taking place in the United States, jobs in the public sector were extremely attractive. They offered security, local prestige, and the prospect of a pension. In 1908, the Civil Service Commission provided an overview of why the public service had proved so attractive to generations of Canadians since the 1840's and drew particular attention to the relationship between social conditions and employment in the public service:

> Owing to the small mileage of railways and to the lack of communications, most of the necessities of life raised in the different localities were consumed locally. Butter, eggs, meats, foodstuffs and articles entering into daily consumption were produced in the locality in which they were consumed. The same characteristic feature was applicable to domestic servants employed in the households of officials in the public service. A generation ago there was no means by which the farmers' daughters could remove easily from the locality in which they were born, and as the supply of domestic servants was greater than the demand, the wages were comparatively small . . . . The civil servant in those days, although not in receipt of a large income had his wants satisfied cheaply and without stint.[105]

Even as late as 1911, employees in the public service still thought in terms of the "dignity" and "respectability" of their position in society.[106] Norman Ward has pointed out that the system worked very nicely for the politicians themselves as they moved from Parliament to patronage posts. Professor Ward, who has studied these matters in greater detail than any other scholar, concluded that politics was by no means "the precarious profession it is often assumed to be. Until very recently, only a small number of private businesses were in a position to provide positions for 30% of their employees."[107] For most of the 1848-1910 period, then, prevailing social and economic circumstances made the ever-increasing number of jobs at the disposal of government an immense reservoir of attractive, secure, and locally prestigious employment. It was no accident that patronage began to lose some of its intensity as the Canadian economy began to grow rapidly and diversify in the transforming 1900-1930 years.

There was yet another related characteristic of Canadian society that contributed to the successful working of the patronage system—the important position in society occupied by the professional middle classes. The link between political patronage and the size and status of this class was most clearly established in Quebec. With the advent of responsible government, government was in the hands of party leaders who depended on the Quebec anchor, and this dependence allowed the Quebec professional classes to come into their own. Jacques Monet has described the process at its origins in the 1840's and 1850's:

> The Canadian professional class had been struggling to secure an outlet for its ambitions: so now with a kind of bacterial thoroughness it began to invade every vital organ of government and divide up among its members hundreds of posts as Judges, Queen's Counsels, Justices of the Peace, Medical Examiners, school inspectors, militia captains, postal clerks, mail conductors, census commissioners. And as the flatteries and salaries of office percolated down to other classes in society — from merchants who wanted seats on the Legislative Council down to impoverished habitants on the crowded seigneuries — the Canadians came to realise how parliamentary democracy could be more than a lovely ideal. It was also a profitable fact."[108]

This process was embedded during the Union and flourished in the expanding post-Confederation patronage world. "La classe dirgeante" in Quebec was the professional nobility born of the people which had succeeded the title of nobility ["la noblesse professionelle, née du peuple et qui a succedé a la noblesse titre"].[109] Insofar as there was a bourgeoisie in nineteenth-century Quebec, it was this class of upper- and lower-middle class professionals and not a bourgeoisie created by industrial capitalism. The invigorating lifeblood of this class was supplied by the political parties and their patronage. They turned to political leaders like LaFontaine, Cartier, Mercier and Laurier for influence and rewards. Whether they belonged to that section of the professional middle classes who looked to the exterior, predominantly English pole of federal politics or whether they contented themselves with remaining local notables, they were intimately tied to the political parties. Between the politicians and the professionals, osmosis was continual ["l'osmose fut constante"].[110] Jean-Charles Bonenfant has set out a typical pattern of increasing social status through politics — the political man came from a comfortable bourgeois background, usually received education for the law, got himself elected to the lower house to end up as legislative councillor, senator or judge ["l'homme politique était bourgeois d'une certaine aisance, ayant de preférénce une formation juridique, se faisant élire à la chambre basse pour mourir plus tard conseiller législatif, senateur ou juge."][111] This configuration of social class and social trends, combined with traditional statist values, created ideal conditions for the effective deployment of government patronage in Quebec after the 1840's.

But it is important to recognize that conditions were not all that different in English-Canada during this period. Once again, the differences in Canada compared to Britain and the United States were critical. In the United States, the democratically elected governments of an expanding society and economy had similar room for manoeuvre, but in that country the vibrant, gigantic capitalist economy created other influential centres of power that reduced or circumvented the reach of government. In Canada, the party in office faced no such powerful outside rivals. The Ottawa River was not a dividing line with respect to these social and political patterns. The mobility patterns, values and social aspirations of the English- and French-Canadian middle classes were remarkably similar between the 1840's and 1910.

Conditions were not identical. In the anglophone provinces, there were more varied responses to business, commerce and the world of finance and banking, but before industrialization and the accompanying urbanization took hold in the decade after 1900, English-Canada was a rural, localized and churched society that was tinged only in places by the secular and transforming world of industrial capitalism. It was a society in which the most prestigious groups belonged to the professional middle classes. "The Canadian middle class," the sociologist S.D. Clark has observed, "has grown up very largely within a bureaucratic structure of power."[112] It was a society in which patronage was a normal route to sought-after positions from customs officials to county judges that conferred varying degrees of security and local status. English Canadians, like their counterparts in Quebec, turned to the patronage of the party in power to become judges, senators, QCs, medical examiners, postal and customs officials, and a range of other offices in the public service. The operation of these social processes may have been less intense outside Quebec, more related to business and commercial activity, but the fact remains that there were profound similarities between English and French Canadians. There was a fundamental convergence between both groups on the nature of politics and the ramifications of party patronage. On patronage, English and French Canadians spoke different dialects but the same language.

One final factor must be brought into the picture to explain why patronage loomed so large in Canadian political culture. The party leaders in Ottawa used patronage as a major tool to tackle the problem of regionalism. The growth of federal government activity in Manitoba, British Columbia and the Northwest Territories obviously enabled Macdonald and later Laurier to use the public service to consolidate local party organizations. But even in the established setting of the Maritime Provinces, patronage was in the vanguard of federal policy as a means to quiet regional discontent with national policies. Macdonald's agreement with Joseph Howe to bring the

leading anti-confederate into the Conservative cabinet and allow him to
supervise patronage deployment in Nova Scotia marked the beginnings of
this approach to those irritating Maritime complaints. As J. Murray Beck,
after making the most exhaustive analysis so far of Macdonald's efforts to
pacify the antis and their successor critics, has drily observed, "patronage
remained his handiest weapon to get the Nova Scotian MPs to give reasonable support to the government." Throughout the 1870's and 1880's, as Peter
Waite has described, patronage disbursement remained the modus operandi
of federal cabinet ministers as they continued their efforts to pacify the
Maritimes.[113] It was all these basic social and economic circumstances that
enabled the federal political parties of Macdonald and Laurier to make
patronage such a pervasive and powerful organizing force in Canadian
society and politics.

The matter of patronage and the Maritimes leads directly to a central
question about Canadian political development that was raised in the introduction and early part of this chapter. I have argued that the advent of
responsible government in the Union of the Canadas during the 1840's led to
party government, characterized by intense use of patronage. Yet the colonies of Nova Scotia and New Brunswick, not to mention other white settlement colonies such as the Cape and the Australian colonies, all experienced
this transition from crown rule to party rule. In all these cases, certainly in
the case of Nova Scotia, this transition was accompanied by new party
government and by that new party government working the public service
through patronage. But all these other cases turned out differently from the
Canadian one. In Nova Scotia, patronage was disbursed after responsible
government, but it was a more moderate, administrative use of patronage.
Joseph Howe never took to patronage like a duck to water until he came into
Macdonald's pond after Confederation. Howe, according to Beck, "regarded
the appointing power as the least pleasant of his official duties."[114] This is
somewhat of a surprise for such an inveterate office-seeker himself, but the
clue to the puzzle is that Howe still had a British outlook on politics. In a
revealing case, he refused to do anything for Dr. Slocumb, "his ally in
organising the electoral victory in Lunenburg which had made responsible
government possible." This was exactly the type of person Macdonald
rewarded in Canada—patronage should not be wasted on mere friends but
should be given to those who worked hard for the party. In replying to
Slocumb's complaints, Howe explained that if Slocumb expected members
of the legislature to "do acts which they could justify upon no principle
recognised in . . . British communities, all I can say is that I never so
understood it."[115] There it was. Obviously patronage had its place; Howe, in
particular, expected offices to be doled out to friends for that was the only
way government could operate in those times. But Howe still believed he was

in a "British community," and he stopped short of making rigorous use of patronage for partisan ends over a long period of years. Howe had no long game to play in this respect. Therein lay the difference between Nova Scotia and Canada.

But in this same respect, Canada had ceased to be a British community by the 1850's, as governors from Elgin to Dufferin to Minto observed when they compared Canadian and British politics. The difference in Canada (both as a Union and then a Confederation) was that patronage was used in a much more rigorous, hard-headed way to build up party strength and permanently weaken the opposition. The reasons for this difference, as we have seen, had to do with conditions in the Canadas from the 1760's to the 1840's. In the Canadas, the politics during the transition to responsible government were more bitter, divisive, and physically violent than in any other British colony. Responsible government had been a much more dramatic and traumatic experience in Canada. Because of that experience, for the next fifty years Conservatives regarded the opposition as tainted with treason. Parties talked about their opponents as "the enemy." In these conditions, the party in power felt it morally and constitutionally legitimate to use patronage to the utmost extent to establish themselves and undermine the opposition. Party had to be built up at all costs, and few holds were barred against the tainted opposition foe. Outside observers were struck by the bitterness of partisan rhetoric in Canada and by the fury of electioneering. The French political scientist André Siegfried gave as his informed view in 1900 that Canadian politics were exceptional because of the fury of party battles.[116]

Siegfried also noted that in Canada, the "principle preoccupation of parties | was | their own existence. In Canada, the party is almost a sacred institution—it is held in esteem almost like one's religion."[117] This was a peculiar development of Canada, a development that was not duplicated with the same intensity in Nova Scotia or any other white settlement colony that received responsible government. It was not accidental that the first systematic condemnation of the Canadian patronage system, apart from the critiques of intellectuals like Goldwin Smith and William de la Sueur in the 1880's and 1890's, came after 1900 from the new prairie provinces and from Robert Borden, the Nova Scotian leader of the Conservatives.[118] All colonies took the same kind of medicine to make responsible government work; in Canada, it was an exceptionally strong brew.

But this strong brew worked, and perhaps in a setting like Canada's, with its lack of ethnic homogeneity and its sheer size, only such unusually intense methods of securing party solidity would have worked. It was easy for academics and intellectuals like Goldwin Smith, Daniel Wilson and William de la Sueur to deplore what they saw as the corrupting influence of Macdonaldian approach to politics. But the methods were successful and achieved a breakthrough in Canadian politics—they produced political stability. Just as it misses the point to concentrate on Walpole's methods of corruption and influence in England from 1722 to 1742, while ignoring the relationship of these methods to the emergence of modern political stability in Britain, so too it must be acknowledged that in Canada, patronage played a central role in building up a disciplined majority party that, in contrast to all its predecessors, was able to run effective administrations. To use that old sociologists' phrase, patronage played a critical functional role in Canada. To adopt the more homely words of a Quebec witness before the Civil Service Commission, it was "une petite peu de graise pour faire marcher la machine."[119] With this stability, British capital began to flow back into Canada; the government was able to carry on a difficult policy of western consolidation and organize policies to help Canada avoid integration into the larger, more successful American economy. The party in power with such tools at its disposal was also able to accommodate the varying interests of the two major ethnic blocs. French Canadians complained about the fate of francophone minority rights outside Quebec and about Canada's role in the Empire; English Canadians complained about the Métis rebel Louis Riel, Catholic influence and French-Canadian disloyalty, but both groups were satisfied by the political system itself. In view of the complex problems in governing a country like Canada, in view of the turmoil and bitterness that had existed up to the 1840's, the achievement of stability was genuinely remarkable success for Canada's distinctive political culture.

4

CONCLUSIONS AND CONSEQUENCES

Canada's political culture, like all other political cultures, is not static. The pattern of Canadian politics that was woven in the troubled 1790-1850 years and that finally produced stability after 1867 began to undergo marked changes by the 1920's.[1] Economic growth led to industrialization and urbanization, the new western provinces became assertive and critical of central Canadian concepts of government and party, the provinces as a group, but especially Ontario and Quebec from the 1920's on, became more insistent on their rights. Within the federal government itself, the increasingly complex challenges of administration put great pressure on the old patronage system for the higher civil service now required experts and specialists. After the 1908 Civil Service Commission report, a great effort was made to ensure that the top levels of the public service in Ottawa did get staffed by high-minded, well-qualified candidates. These efforts, as Jack Granatstein has shown, paid off handsomely by the production of Canada's small but prestigious group of civil service mandarins.[2] So things did change, but patronage persisted. Newspaper stories still discuss patronage lists in Quebec. Aspiring QCs will still tell you that party service is important. Canada (in 1984), along with Britain (1983) and the United States (1984), has had a recent general election, but Canada is the only one of the three where patronage was a major issue. It is still closer to the surface in Canada and more central to Canada's political culture.

This final chapter is not an attempt to summarize all the changes that have taken place since the 1920's, to lay out the trends in modern Canadian politics; rather it is a summation of those characteristics of Canadian political culture produced by the historical circumstances analysed in the three previous chapters. The transformation of Canada from rural, small-town conditions of the nineteenth century to the complex industrial, urban and regional patterns of the twentieth century has produced a wide range of changes in the working of politics. But the case made here is that the impact of the 1790-1850 formative period was so powerful that its momentum left permanent features on the Canadian political landscape.

Placed in a comparative context with Britain and the United States, a context which has included here as an analytical device the court/country model of the eighteenth century Anglo-American political world, Canada had developed a decidedly "court" or statist orientation in her political culture. The radical American alternative to the growth of central government in eighteenth-century Britain, achieved by replacing monarchical with republican government and by making written definitions of discrete executive and legislative spheres to limit the power of central authority, never had much impact in Canada, and although given a brief rhetorical airing in the crisis years of the 1830's, it was decisively rejected in 1837 as the radical rebellions petered out into futility. The "country" ideology that had proved so potent in the American case was only a fringe phenomenon in the Canadian colonies. Both Tories and mainstream Reformers were believers in strong central government similar to the British model.

Indeed, between the 1790's and the 1840's, Canadian Tories developed a system of "court"-style government more extreme than the version that had developed in England by the early nineteenth century. The governors, the appointed councillors, and the whole class of office-holders in both Upper and Lower Canada constituted ruling classes who were trying to build up an immunity to any representative checks on their power and privileges. They used influence to maintain and strengthen their exclusive control of government. They manipulated the franchise and elections to the assembly. They tried in Upper Canada to operate the Anglican church as an established church on the eighteenth-century English model. They used patronage to build up a network of local support throughout the colonies; and as Professor Wise has shown, patronage was the cement that held these ruling elites in their dominant place.[3]

When the Reformers forced this system to change during the 1840's, some important policies were altered, as, for example, when Anglican privilege was dismantled, but the same basic orientation towards government and politics remained in place. So well did the Reform leaders understand the central importance of patronage in Canadian politics that it was on that issue that they challenged Governor Metcalfe in 1844. Without control of government patronage they knew they could not hold on to power as the Family Compact and Chateau Clique had done since the 1790's. Once they were in office, the Reform administrations of Baldwin and LaFontaine between 1848 and 1851 used patronage extensively to reward and encourage supporters, to shore up administration strength in the assembly and in the country, and to build up party commitment in the localities. Throughout the Union period from 1841 to 1867, governments regularly employed electoral manipulation to tilt the balance against opponents, especially during the bitter battles of the 1840's when, for example, polling stations were situated to discourage opposition voters. In addition, the Union years saw a continuation of the pattern established since the 1790's of government taking the leading role in economic development as administrations poured money into the St. Lawrence canals and the Grand Trunk Railway.

This system of patronage, influence, and active government went from strength to strength after Confederation was established in 1867. The new federal government took the leading role in promoting the Canadian Pacific Railway and by the 1880's had gone deeply into debt to sustain its operations. In turn the CPR became a Conservative party preserve as Tory governments used it for patronage purposes. When their turn came after 1896, the Liberal party did the same with the Canadian Northern Railway.[4] Various official reports throughout the 1867-1914 period show that partisan patronage was endemic throughout the whole giant system of public works that developed after 1867. As the Civil Service Commissioners wrote in 1908, "organization, discipline, zeal for the public service are all conspicuous by their absence . . . . It seems to have been true under all administrations . . . the result of evil methods and practices persisted in for many years."[5] Nor was all this done uncomprehendingly by political leaders. They understood what they were about. When towards the end of his long political career, John A. Macdonald succeeded in getting the 1885 Franchise Act through Parliament, he called it "the greatest triumph" of his life. The legislation enabled his administration to appoint revising offices to scrutinize and validate voters' lists, thus (Macdonald hoped) giving his party the "influence" he thought necessary for continued hold on power in Ottawa. It is surely significant that Macdonald, not given to displays of self-congratulation, should single out this act as his greatest achievement.[6] By doing so, he illustrated where the centre of gravity in Canadian political culture was located.

An integral element of this "court" or statist government and political development was the type of party leadership that emerged during and after the 1840's. During the political struggles of the 1830's and 1840's, the British governors in their increasingly desperate efforts to stave off the Reformers undertook a whole range of mixed executive and political actions. They tried to rally the Tory-Conservative party, they distributed patronage for this partisan end, and they interfered in elections and used their executive power to change electoral boundaries and polling stations. As was written of Lord

Sydenham, these governors did "everything by themselves." The politicians who took over the executive from these governors, beginning with William Draper in 1844 then Baldwin, LaFontaine, Macdonald, Mowat, and Laurier followed the practices of the governors for the same political reasons. Macdonald did everything himself and knew that this made him a different kind of party leader than those in mid-Victorian Britain. He tried to stay in as much personal control of patronage as possible, he raised and spent election funds, and he manipulated electoral boundaries and the franchise. As he told Carnarvon in 1873, much of the work he did as party leader and prime minister in Canada would have been left to the Carlton and Reform Club political organizers in Britain. He was, in fact, as a result of the way the political debate of the 1840's was resolved, taking over both the governor's executive powers as well as being party leader in the assembly.

This is why Goldwin Smith's comparison of Macdonald to that great eighteenth-century deployer of patronage and influence, Robert Walpole, was so insightful. Just as Walpole straddled the worlds of court and Parliament, so Macdonald derived weight and influence from the combining of gubernatorial and party leader functions. When Macdonald returned from a visit to Britain in 1881, one correspondent welcomed him back as "the Prince of Canada . . . |who| has friends numbered by the thousand who are most demonstrative in their joy at his being home because of the offices in his gift to bestow." The writer hoped Macdonald would not think he was angling for place or favours, but he added that he was petitioning on behalf of "our friend J.A. Simpson for Deputy Judge here or a similar appointment in any other county."[7] Because he had seen how the old ruling elites had deployed patronage for personal or cliquish ends rather than to build up an organized following in the localities, Macdonald believed it essential to insist to cabinet colleagues and MPs that patronage be used to build up party loyalty and party electoral readiness. He worked hard to implement this efficient use of patronage through the 1850's and had certainly succeeded by the 1880's. In the long run, Macdonald was unable to prevent the Montreal and Quebec regions of the Conservative party from internecine competition over patronage, nor could he prevent D'Alton McCarthy's Protestant movement from splitting the party in Ontario in the late-1880's, but had Macdonald not tried so singlemindedly to keep on top of things himself, the situation might have slipped out of joint much earlier.

The result of all this—the role of the governors in the 1830's and 1840's, the role of party leaders (above all Macdonald) after 1849—was the emergence in Canada of strong, one-man dominance in leadership of the ruling political party. As Hugh Macdonald wrote to his father in January 1891, there was "practically no Conservative party in Canada at the present time. There is a strong 'John A' party but many of the members of which this is comprised acknowledge allegiance to none of your colleagues and I fear a process of rapid disintegration will set in when anyone else takes command." This filial assessment has been endorsed by the foremost modern scholar of this period, Peter Waite, who has concluded after years of meticulous research and sage writing that "Macdonald, so to speak, was the only principle the Conservative party ever had."[8] This type of leadership became a characteristic feature of Canadian political culture as post-Confederation Canada was ruled by a series of dominant prime ministers—Macdonald (1867-74, 1878-91), Laurier (1896-1911), King (1921-26, 1926-30, 1935-48), St. Laurent (1948-57), and Trudeau (1968-84). A range of circumstances determined the nature and longevity of each of these men's rule, but the starting point of this Canadian political tradition can be traced to the 1840's when party leaders fought successfully to take over the wide-ranging authority of the governors. Because the political battles were so bitter in Canada and both Tory and Reform leaders needed desperately to create and build party strength in the localities, the party leaders had few compunctions about using gubernatorial powers of patronage, influence and electoral manipulation to strengthen their own position and so become dominant figures.

By the middle of the nineteenth century, Canada seemed clearly to have developed a statist system of government. In terms of government's reach into society, in terms of party leadership, and in terms of endemic and pervasive patronage, Canada was far removed from the small, frugal and spare government and political system of classical "country" ideology. In this sense, she had marked out a different pattern from the British and American ones. Patronage to be sure was certainly an important feature of British and American political life in the mid-nineteenth century, but in Canada it was much more openly entrenched as a legitimate activity. Richard Jones's comprehensive assessment of patronage in British politics concludes that as a cement for parties, patronage was declining markedly from the 1840's and was not significant by 1870.[9] Moreover, in Victorian England with its deferential society and its national ruling class, patronage as it continued to operate was just as much a social phenomenon as a political one as jobs were given to those with the right connections. Patronage in the United States was perhaps closer to Canada's version in this respect, but the sheer size and variety of the nineteenth-century American democracy and economy meant that no counterpart of Macdonald would have the time or the energy to scrutinize its use so carefully. Moreover, while patronage was a thoroughgoing feature of American political life no political leader could, as Macdonald did in Canada, justify patronage on the basis of the constitution. Elsewhere, defences were made on the grounds that job rotation was good for the health of democracy, but in Canada Macdonald could openly defend patronage on the grounds that Canada's version of the monarchical constitution gave the party in power the right to appoint its supporters to public offices throughout the land. In this context, Canada had produced in Macdonald a party leader whose philosophy was a combination of Alexander Hamilton's and Robert Walpole's views of government and the working of politics.

If the analysis were stopped at this point, it would seem the statist type of government had comprehensively won out in Canada. But this did not happen. There were powerful countervailing forces working against the triumph of a national government. Once again, the French Canadians were a key factor. Their vote during the 1840's was the single most important factor in forcing power out of the hands of the governor into the hands of party leaders. Macdonald's power rested on the French-Canadian vote between 1867 and 1891. Yet at the same time as the French-Canadian vote gave strength to party leaders like Macdonald and to the administrations he ran, the French Canadians were ever-ready to prevent the overgrowth of federal government power lest it intervene in Quebec and undermine the francophone and Catholic nation in that province. Perhaps even more important in the mid- and late nineteenth century than the French-Canadian roadblock towards too mighty central government was the roadblock thrown up by Ontario. The Liberals were weak at the national level, frustrated by their inability to dethrone Macdonald, their efforts weakened in the 1880's by the timid intellectual leadership of Edward Blake. But if they could not counteract Macdonald in Ottawa, they could in Ontario, the most populous and prosperous province. The leader of the Ontario Liberal party, Oliver Mowat came from the same background as Macdonald and shared his approach towards government and politics. As soon as Mowat came to power in Ontario, he increased the size of government and began distributing patronage in the same comprehensive and singleminded manner of Macdonald. Mowat's government fought Ottawa to increase the realm of provincial government—most famously over the issuing of liquor licences, a matter of immense political consequence in the localities where taverns were meeting-places of considerable influence, but also over a whole range of economic development matters.

Thus, although the party in power in Ottawa did have great reach into society and did reign over an ever-increasing state apparatus of railways, public works, and public service, it was limited because the French Canadians balked at tendencies towards central intervention and because the Mowat-led Liberals in Ontario were able to build up a provincial duplicate and rival to Macdonald's party-state in Ottawa. While the central Canadian government was "court" in style, it could not pull off the final triumph envisaged by Macdonald when he dreamed of the provinces declining into mere municipalities. In this context the Tories of the 1840's had been proved wrong. They had argued that by destroying the power of the governor and the appointed councils, all power would be thrown into the hands of party leaders in the assembly who would then be able to build up an unchallenged partisan-government. The assemblies, argued Tory critics, would possess "a power superior to that of the House of Commons, the House of Representatives or any other body we know of short of despotic authority."[10] But these Tory doomsayers were unable to imagine the possibility that new provinces could act as counterweights to the seemingly limitless reach of central government. Macdonald could not pull off his final triumph because he was faced with rival "court" governments in Ontario and Quebec.

As other provinces grew, they benefited from these developments. Provincial leaders expanded their bureaucracies and fought politically and judicially to expand their spheres of influence.[11] From the very beginning then, battle was joined between the federal government and the provincial governments. In the modern period, these historical traditions have culminated in periodic federal-provincial conferences which negotiate major decisions about the running of Canada. The great clue to the distinctiveness of Canada's political culture lies in this development. The "country" challenge to "court" orientation was paltry, but rival "court" governments in the provinces did the job of circumscribing central power.

One of the unfortunate consequences of Canada's political development during and after the 1840's was that most party workers and most MPs remained very local and parochial in their outlook. Canadian society was localistic simply because of prevailing economic, demographic, and communications conditions through most of the nineteenth century. The political parties did not create localistic attitudes, but by their use of them, they entrenched localism in the Canadian political tradition. Between the 1790's and the 1840's, the ruling elites in Upper and Lower Canada consisted of a series of local notables connected by patronage and influence. When the Reform and Conservative party leaders took over in the 1840's, they were desperate to establish their party strength in each locality. To do this they channelled patronage to party worthies and local party activists. It became a hallmark of the system that local patronage could only be given to local men. It was hard for even Macdonald or Laurier to break this pattern, so fixed had it become. "I need not tell you," wrote Prime Minister Laurier as late as 1896, "that it is always difficult to bring an outsider into a locality."[12] After its exhaustive investigation of patronage in the public service, the Civil Service Commission concluded that "each locality is separately guarded."[13] William LeSueur, a knowledgeable critic who had actually worked in the public service since 1851 (and was secretary of the post office from 1888 to 1902), despaired of the system. "Localism," he declared in exasperation, "is rampant . . . MPs know that the special interests of his constituency not the general interests of the country are those over which he has to watch with the greatest vigilance and for his dealings with which he will be held to the strictest account."[14]

Accompanying this intense localism was another characteristic of Canadian politics that outsiders immediately noticed. The language of Canadian politics was exceptionally bitter. Lord Elgin was struck by this aspect of Canadian political life in the tumultuous late 1840's, which is not surprising, but in 1874 another governor, Lord Dufferin, was still discouraged to see that "party spirit runs so high and is so unscrupulous." And at the turn of the century André Siegfried observed that Canada was unusual for the bitter fury aroused between parties.[15] The origins of this feature of Canada's political landscape can again be traced back to the critical 1790-1850 years. Between the 1790's and the 1830's, Reform critics, understandably frustrated by the abuses of power employed by the privileged elites to maintain their hold on government and influence, easily slid into more extreme language. Then, following the 1837 rebellions, the Tories and Conservatives were convinced that any opposition to established authority bordered on treason. For their part, once they came to power in 1848, the Reform leaders believed the Tories were intent on destroying the legitimacy of the entire responsible government concept. After 1867, Macdonald genuinely believed that continued opposition to his Conservative coalition government was near to disloyalty. Thus, from the very beginning of organized politics in Canada, the loyalty and treason cry was raised. This imputation of disloyalty to the opposition endorsed the government view that patronage should be given exclusively to its loyal partisans and gave currency to unthinking, accusatory political dialogue. This was all part of what one observer in the 1880's described as "an overgrowth of partyism."[16]

To all this it might well be objected that localism and partisan rancour were features of British and American political life in the nineteenth century. This must be conceded, but a case can still be made that localism and partyism were in the long run more corrosive in Canada because Canada's complex circumstances required more constructive thinking among politicians and MPs. In the British case, the existence of a national ruling class, the persistence of social deference, the tradition that MPs were not mere delegates, the slow intrusion of democratic standards of judgment, all meant that MPs were not so intensely local in outlook as their counterparts in Canada and the United States. This is not to say that they were broadminded or statesmanlike for they were certainly blinkered by class preconceptions, but they did not have to preoccupy themselves so intently with their localities as Canadian MPs did. In the case of the United States, the existence of a national ideology stemming from the revolution, an ideology that was given a unitary definition after the South's defeat in the Civil War, and the iconolatry of the presidency created national symbols over and above the petty doings of Congressmen. In the case of Canada, such a national ruling class or such a group of national symbols did not exist.

When English Canadians seized on imperialism between the 1880's and 1914 as a means of defining their identity and giving themselves a sense of power in the world, this growth of nationalist sentiment only deepened divisions between English and French Canadians. Nor did the Canadian Senate help in this respect. Far from becoming an upper house that might rise above political parochialism, it was a chamber entirely composed of patronage appointments reflecting partisan needs.[17] It never became a forum for defining and nurturing Canadian national values. In these conditions everything depended on the federal parties, from MPs in Ottawa to the hundreds of party notables and activists throughout the localities. And the party system that was produced by the 1790-1850 formative period did only a mediocre job.

Its one great achievement was to produce political stability. That achievement should not be underestimated in a country like Canada, where civil and political discord had characterized colonial development for half a century before Confederation. The political stability achieved enabled English and French Canadians to accommodate their interests and the new Confederation to work. Perhaps that is all that ought to be expected, but it is reasonable to go on and make the point that the Canadian federal party system did little that was constructive or imaginative on the fundamental issue in Canada — the relationship of French and English Canadians.

A telling example of this is language use in the federal public service. It was obviously necessary that public servants work in French and English, but no attempt was made to structure the system in ways that would encourage and reward language expertise. William LeSueur described how the system worked:

> In a service where two languages are used it is obviously unfair that a man who brings to the Service a knowledge of both and is made use of by the Department in which he serves, should derive no advantage whatsoever from that fact. In the Department in which I serve a man who knows both French and English is made to do work requiring a knowledge of both these languages and to do it for his seniors. A senior clerk may send to a junior clerk that portion of his work which requires knowledge of a second language and the junior gets nothing at all in the way of promotion for this special qualification.[18]

The bilingual clerk got no recognition because both federal parties (and both English- and French-Canadian party leaders) were interested in the public service only in terms of party patronage. What was true in 1877 was still true in 1907, when the Civil Service Commission reported that partisanship in appointments and promotions was the dominant characteristic of the public service. In this critical area of national activity, the political culture that had emerged from the 1840's meant that there were artificial barriers to any potential expansion of language duality. Had the parties not been so obsessed with their influence and with their patronage strategy for building up loyalty and electoral readiness, the public service of Canada might have accepted much earlier, and in a more formal manner, that bilingual merit deserved systematic reward because of its own internal needs. Here then we can see how the tools that produced stability also produced constraints.

The great paradox lying at the heart of Canadian political culture is that the very methods which produced such a successful stability at the same time encouraged localism and discouraged any constructive thinking on French-Canadian, English-Canadian relations. Kenneth McRae, in a thoughtful discussion of how Arend Lijphart's (the Dutch political scientist who is an expert on politics in segmented societies) model of consociational democracy applies to Canada, has argued that "even by the most charitable interpretation, the political system's capacity to learn and adapt to linguistic-cultural diversity has not been high." The federal parties have been unable to work out policies on "the race question" but have produced, instead, conditions of immobilization and stalemate. McCrae concludes that the Canadian system has a low learning capacity,[19] and LeSueur, back in 1877, would certainly have agreed. In this context then, the Canadian political culture that formed after the 1840's produced parties that were political dinosaurs— they had great weight and presence throughout society, but they had small brains. From the time that modern party formation began in the 1840's, Canada's political culture encouraged only the party leader/ prime minister and perhaps one or two lieutenants to take long-term national interests into account.

The federal parties, in fact, have become increasingly ineffective, as many basic issues are now dealt with at the periodic federal-provincial conferences and in the regular, bureaucratic dialogue between Ottawa and the provinces. The federal parties were the only arena in Canada where English and French Canadians came together in an ongoing manner.[20] In the favourable conditions from 1864 to 1910, they achieved success by creating stability in a country that had proved difficult to govern, but the very features which made them so effective in that period, made the parties leaden-footed when the rise of provincial rights and the growth of modern nationalism in Quebec demanded more imaginative and constructive solutions. If it is true that the fate of any federation "depends on the nature of the party system that develops," then the Canadian federal parties have a lot to be proud of but also much to answer for.[21] The historical origins of the national parties had ill-prepared them for seeking solutions to Canada's fundamental problems. Back in 1880, J.C. Dent remarked of John A. Macdonald that it was his "misfortune to enter political life under auspices unfavourable to the speedy enlargement of his mind."[22] What was true for Macdonald's nascence as a politician was true for the birth of Canadian political culture as a whole. The political culture of Macdonald's and Laurier's Canada was a flowering of the seeds planted in the troubled 1791-1849 years. It was a flourishing growth of a peculiarly Canadian version of monarchical-party government, a growth that was a final working out of constitutional and political trends since the 1790's rather than a useful preparation for Canada's complex problems in the twentieth century.

But this is to end on too judgmental a note. By making comprehensive use of statist techniques, the federal administrations of Macdonald and Laurier between 1867 and 1911 built up their reach and influence and brought stability to a country whose course since 1790 had been singularly fractious and violent. The French-Canadian governments in Quebec and the powerful provincial regimes in Ontario duplicated the statist techniques in a successful effort to prevent an overwhelming central power from emerging, and by so doing they entrenched the "court" orientation at both levels of the new Confederation. If the political culture of the United States can be traced back to its "country" origins in the eighteenth century, so too Canada's political culture can be traced back to the "court" counterpart of that "country" ideology—to the "court" or statist political tradition legitimized by Robert Walpole and his successors in the eighteenth and early nineteenth centuries. The wedding of this statist orientation derived from the British and colonial past to North American social conditions has created the fascinating paradoxes and complexities that lie at the centre of modern Canadian political culture.

NOTES

NOTES TO THE INTRODUCTION

1. Bernard Bailyn, *The Origins of American Politics* (New York, 1968).
2. Jack P. Greene, *The Quest For Power: The Lower Houses of Assembly in the Southern Royal Colonies 1689-1776* (Chapel Hill, 1963).
3. John M. Murrin, "The Great Inversion, or Court versus Country: a Comparison of the Revolutionary Settlements in England (1688-1721) and America (1776-1816)," in J.G.A. Pocock, ed., *Three British Revolutions 1641, 1688, 1776* (Princeton, 1980), pp. 368-453.
4. Ibid., p. 425.
5. Louis Hartz, *The Liberal Tradition in America* (New York, 1955); Louis Hartz, et al., *The Founding of New Societies* (New York, 1964).
6. Gad Horowitz, "Conservatism, Liberalism and Socialism in Canada: an Interpretation," *Canadian Journal of Economics and Political Science (CJEPS)* 32 (1966).
7. Kenneth McCrac, "The Structure of Canadian History," in Hartz, et al., *The Founding of New Societies* argues that "Canada offers almost a classic instance of a two fragment society." The most ambitious effort to relate the Hartz approach to modern Canadian political culture is David Bell and Lorne Tepperman, *The Roots of Disunity* (Toronto, 1979), a book that combines the political science approach with that of the historian.
8. There is an extensive literature on all of these cases. A convenient summary is provided in a recent survey of British Empire history which places the white settlement colonies on centre stage after 1783: T.O. Lloyd, *The British Empire 1558-1983* (Oxford, 1984), pp. 163-69, 187-89, 198-200, 284-87, 306-12, 393-94.
9. W.P.M. Kennedy, *Documents on the Canadian Constitution 1795-1915* (Toronto, 1918), pp. 149-50, 207-20. The proceeds from the Quebec Revenue Act formed the largest single part of the total revenue. There were other sources of revenue (beginning in 1795) derived from provincial statutes, the appropriation of which the assembly fought to control. The crown revenues began to fall behind government needs; this led to a sharp and prolonged struggle between governors and assemblies over the appropriation of provincially raised revenues. The crown revenues (along with designated appropriations from provincial statutes) were large enough for governors to try to go it alone and refuse to give in to assembly demands. In this respect, the Canadian governors were in a much stronger position than their counterparts in colonial America before the revolution. For a still unsurpassed account of all this, see D.G. Creighton, "The Struggle for Financial Control in Lower Canada 1818-1831," *Canadian Historical Review. CHR* 12 (1931): 120-44.
10. The best coverage, summing up the spe-

cialist literature, is provided by the Canadian Centenary Series. For this period, the volumes are Hilda Neatby, *Quebec 1760-1791: The Revolutionary Age* (Toronto, 1966), Gerald M. Craig, *Upper Canada, 1784-1841: The Formative Years* (Toronto, 1963), J.M.S. Careless, *The Union of the Canadas 1841-1857: The Growth of Canadian Institutions* (Toronto, 1967) and W.L. Morton, *The Critical*

Years: The Union of British North America 1857-1873 (Toronto, 1964) along with Fernand Ouellet, *Histoire Sociale et Economique du Quebec 1760-1850* (Montreal, 1966).

11. Carl Berger, *The Writing of Canadian History* (Toronto, 1976), p. 259.

12. H.J. Hanham, "Canadian History in the 1970's, *CHR* 63 (1977): p.3.

NOTES TO CHAPTER 1

1. J.E. Collins, *Life and Times of the Rt. Hon. Sir John A. Macdonald* (Toronto, 1883), pp. 543ff. During a debate in the Canadian legislature, Macdonald referred to "the great Mr. Pitt" and chided the Reform administration with having "Walpoles in the ministry, not Pitts." See also J. Pennington Macpherson, *Life of the Rt. Hon. John A. Macdonald* (St. John, N.B., 1891), I, p. 261. Egerton Ryerson, during the heated political controversies over responsible government, turned for guidance to the relationship of Pitt and George III in 1784. See Egerton Ryerson, *The Story of My Life* (Toronto, 1884), p. 334. On Macdonald's admiration of Edmund Burke and his cleaving to Burkean views of politics and government, see Rod Preece, "The Political Wisdom of Sir John A. Macdonald," *Canadian Journal of Political Science* 17 (1984):459-86.

2. Gerald M. Craig, *Upper Canada: The Formative Years 1784-1841* (Toronto, 1963), pp. 20-32.

3. Dufferin to Carnarvon, Ottawa, 13 March 1874 and 9 October 1877, and Carnarvon to Dufferin, Newbury, 28 August 1877, in C.W. DeKiewiet, ed., *The Dufferin-Carnarvon Correspondence* (Toronto, 1955), pp. 2, 365.

4. The following comparison between English and American developments after 1688 is based on the illuminating work of John M. Murrin, "The Great Inversion," pp. 368-453.

5. J.R. Jones, *Country and Court: England 1658-1714* (Cambridge, MA, 1979), pp. 8-44, 197-98, 217, 234-35.

6. Murrin, "The Great Inversion," pp. 379-80. Jones *Country and Court*, pp. 234-35, points out that James II, even had he achieved his plans, would still have been in a weaker position than Louis XIV.

7. Jones, *Country and Court*, pp. 234-54.

8. Murrin, "The Great Inversion," pp. 381-82.

9. Ibid., 381; Jones, *Country and Court*, pp. 316-56.

10. W.A. Speck, *Stability and Strife: England 1714-1760* (Cambridge, MA, 1979), pp. 11-30; Caroline Robbins, *The Eighteenth Century Commonwealthman* (London, 1959); Bernard Bailyn, *The Ideological Origins of the American Revolution* (Cambridge, MA, 1967), pp. 35-37.

11. J.H. Plumb, *The Growth of Political Stability in England 1675-1725* (London, 1967).

12. Murrin, "The Great Inversion," pp. 381-82, points out that "England's Revolution Settlement created a centralised system of Court politics and one party rule"; Speck, *Stability and Strife*, pp. 20-22. This national government, however, kept its hands off local government in the counties.

13. E. Neville Williams, *The Eighteenth Century Constitution 1688-1815* (Cambridge, 1960), pp. 75-76.

14. Lewis Namier, *The Structure of Politics at the Accession of George III* (London, 1929) and *England in the Age of the American Revolution* (London, 1930). See too the excellent recent synthesis by Speck, *Stability & Strife 1714-1760*.

15. Norman Gash, *Aristocracy and the People: England 1815-1865* (Cambridge, MA, 1979), pp. 1-128; Frank O'Gorman, *The Emergence of the British Two-Party System 1760-1832* (London, 1982).

16. A.D. Harvey, *Britain in the Early Nineteenth Century* (New York, 1978).

17. G.B. Finlayson, *England in the 1830's: Decade of Reform* (London, 1969); Oliver MacDonagh, *Early Victorian Government 1830-1870* (London, 1977); W.L. Lubenow, *The Politics of Government Growth* (Newton Abbot, 1971). This, however, was accompanied by a withdrawal of the

national government from management of the economy that had been the pattern under the old trade and navigation system of the seventeenth and eighteenth centuries.

18. Murrin, "The Great Inversion," p. 411.
19. Bailyn, *The Origins of American Politics.*
20. Bernard Bailyn, *The Ordeal of Thomas Hutchinson* (Cambridge, MA, 1974), pp. 78-79.
21. William Blackstone, *Commentaries on the Laws of England,* 15th ed. (London, 1809), I, p. 153; Williams, *The Eighteenth Century Constitution,* pp. 67-135.
22. John Adams to Abigail Adams, 30 June 1774 and 5 July 1774, in L.H. Butterfield, ed., *The Adams Family Correspondence* (Cambridge, MA, 1963), I, pp. 116-17, 124-25; Page Smith, *John Adams* (New York, 1962), I, pp. 133-34.
23. Greene, *The Quest for Power, passim.*
24. Murrin, "The Great Inversion," pp. 384-85.
25. Bailyn, *Ideological Origins of the American Revolution,* pp. 22-54.
26. Gordon S. Wood, *The Creation of the American Republic* (Chapel Hill, 1969), pp. 143-50.
27. Murrin, "The Great Inversion," pp. 407-11.
28. S.F. Wise, "Colonial Attitudes From the Era of the War of 1812 to the Rebellions of 1837," in S.F. Wise and R.C. Brown, *Canada Views the United States: Nineteenth Century Political Attitudes* (Toronto, 1967), pp. 16-43. H.S Fox to Sir George Arthur, Washington, 6 December 1838, in Charles R. Sanderson, ed., *The Arthur Papers* (Toronto, 1957), I, p. 420.
29. Eric Foner, *Politics and Ideology in the Age of the Civil War* (New York, 1980), pp. 10-11, 32-33, 34-37, 53.
30. Murrin, "The Great Inversion," pp. 425-26.
31. Gordon Stewart and George Rawlyk, *The Nova Scotia Yankees and the American Revolution* (Toronto, 1972), pp. 13-23.
32. Kennedy, *Documents on the Canadian Constitution,* 136-38. See above, note 9 to the Introduction.
33. This is not to ignore the major debate about the impact of the conquest on French-Canadian society, a quite different issue. On the impact of the conquest see Michel Brunet, *Les Canadiens après la Conquête 1759-1775* (Ottawa, 1969), *passim,* and Fernand Ouellet, *Histoire Economique et Sociale* , pp. 45-168. On French-Canadian views of the British

regime, see Neatby's concise conclusion in *Quebec 1760-1791,* pp. 262-63.
34. Neatby, *Quebec 1760-1791,* pp. 30-44; Ouellet, *Histoire Economique et Sociale,* pp. 92-96.
35. Janice Potter, *The Liberty We Seek: Loyalist Ideology in Colonial New York and Massachusetts* (Cambridge, MA, 1983), pp. 15-61.
36. J.G.A. Pocock, "The Classical Theory of Deference," *American Historical Review* 81 (1976): 516-23.
37. Potter, *Loyalist Ideology,* pp. 119-21; Kenneth A. Lockridge, *Settlement and Unsettlement in Early America: The Crisis of Political Legitimacy before the Revolution* (Cambridge, 1981), pp. 109-10.
38. Craig, *Upper Canada 1791-1841,* pp. 20-41; Kennedy, *Documents on the Canadian Constitution,* pp. 136-38, 207-22. See also note 9 to the Introduction for a discussion of the revenue issue.
39. Grenville to Dorchester, Whitehall, 20 October 1789, *Public Archives of Canada Report* (1890), pp. 11-12; Kennedy, *Documents on the Canadian Constitution,* 208-9; Marcus Van Steen, *Governor Simcoe and His Lady* (Toronto, 1968), p. 41; Edwin C. Guillet, *Pioneer Life in Upper Canada* (Toronto, 1933), p. 617; John Graves Simcoe to Bishop of Quebec, Kingston, 30 April 1795, and Simcoe to Henry Dundas, 6 November 1792, Simcoe Memorandum 28 February 1794, in E.A. Cruikshank, ed., *The Correspondence of Lieutenant-Governor John Graves Simcoe* (Toronto, 1923), 1, pp. 251-52; 2, p. 167; 3, 348-49.
40. Simcoe to Sir Henry Dundas, 30 June 1791, in Cruikshank, *The Simcoe Correspondence,* 1, p. 31.
41. Craig, *Upper Canada 1791-1841,* 31-32. For other criticisms of the executive see "Political Conditions in Upper Canada 1806," *Public Archives of Canada Report* (1892), pp. 35-39, 54.
42. Simcoe to Sir Joseph Banks, 8 January 1791, in Cruikshank, *The Simcoe Correspondence,* 1, p. 18; Mattie M. I. Clark, *The Positive Side of John Graves Simcoe* (Toronto, 1943), p. 15; Craig, *Upper Canada 1791-1841,* pp. 20-22.
43. Creighton, "Struggle for Financial Control 1818-1831," p. 127, quoting Dalhousie to Drinkwater, 23 July 1820. The comparison with Great Britain is paraphrased by Creighton.

44. Charles Lucas, ed., *The Durham Report* (Oxford, 1912), 2. p. 73.
45. Ouellet, *Histoire Economique et Sociale*, pp. 194-212; Gilles Paquet and Jean-Pierre Wallot, *Patronage et Pouvoir dans le Bas-Canada 1794-1812* (Montreal, 1973).
46. Fernand Ouellet, "Le Nationalisme Cana-dien-Francais: des ses origines a l'insur-rection de 1837," *CHR* 45 (1964): 277-92.
47. Pacquet and Wallot, *Patronage et Pouvoir 1794-1812*, pp. 35-74.
48. Fernand Ouellet, "Louis-Joseph Papineau," *Dictionary of Canadian Biography* (Tor-onto, 1972), 10, 568-69, 570, 575, 577. Ouellet has some deeply insightful things to say on this matter. He points out, for example, that Papineau viewed the seig-neurial system as a device to divide up landed property between many individuals, thus acting as a brake on monarchical tyranny and as a barrier to urbanization and consequent anglicization. The seig-neur, as Ouellet nicely phrases it, was to serve as "the unremunerated architect of equality"—an almost pure Jeffersonian concept that most in Lower Canada, what-ever language they spoke, found difficult to comprehend. Papineau was also dis-trustful of the Banque du Peuple because of his association of national banks with over-strong centralized government. To the end of his life, Papineau viewed both responsible government and Confedera-tion as hoaxes designed to "perpetuate English monarchical and aristocratic insti-tutions in Canada."
49. W.L. Morton, ed., *Monck Letters and Journals 1863-1868* (Toronto, 1970). Lady Monck wrote that they passed "the old French chateau where lives the ex-rebel Papineau, now become quite loyal. He has lovely gardens to his chateau and a small chapel close to him. I believe he sent a bouquet to the Prince of Wales when he was travelling here (1850)."
50. Ouellet, "Louis-Joseph Papineau," p. 577.
51. Jacques Monet, *The Last Cannon Shot: A Study of French-Canadian Nationalism 1837-1850* (Toronto, 1969), pp. 3, 281, 398. In 1846 Augustin-Norbert Morin wrote "we are in our habits, by our laws, by our religion . . . monarchists and conserva-tives.".
52. Henry Milner, *Politics in the New Quebec* (Toronto, 1978), pp. 19, 85-105.
53. Pacquet and Wallot, *Patronage et Pouvoir 1794-1812*, pp. 137-41.
54. Craig, *Upper Canada 1784-1841*, pp. 188-209; Aileen Dunham, *Political Unrest in Upper Canada 1815-1836* (London, 1927).
55. William Kilbourn, *The Firebrand: Wil-liam Lyon Mackenzie and the Rebellion in Upper Canada* (Toronto, 1956), pp. 154-178.
56. Elgin to Grey, Toronto, 23 March 1850 and 28 June 1851, in A.G. Doughty, ed., *Elgin-Grey Papers* (Ottawa, 1937), pp. 51, 609. One critic of LaFontaine captured this same characteristic of the Reformers of the 1840's when he said of LaFontaine, "il passe dans le public pour se donner des airs aritstocratiques." See Monet, *French-Canadian Nationalism 1837-1850*, p. 59. The *Colonical Gazette*, 21 September 1844 quote is cited in Peter Burroughs, *The Colonial Reformers and Canada 1830-1849*, (Toronto, 1969), p. 169.
57. Sydney W. Jackman, *Galloping Head* (London, 1958); S.F. Wise, ed., *Sir Fran-cis Bond Head: A Narrative* (Toronto, 1969 [1839]). Craig, *Upper Canada 1784-1841*, pp. 232-42. Head raised so many hopes among the reformers simply be-cause he was a civilian governor. See H.T. Manning and J.S. Galbraith, "The Ap-pointment of Francis Bond Head: A New Insight," *CHR* 42 (1961): 50-52.
58. S.F. Wise, "Upper Canadian Conserva-tive Tradition," in Morris Zaslow, *Profiles of a Province* (Toronto, 1967), pp. 26-29. Wise writes that the use of patronage by the ruling groups was "the central fact of provincial politics."
59. Paquet and Wallot, *Patronage et Pouvoir 1794-1812*, pp. 138-39. These authors em-phasize the pervasiveness and centrality of the patronage issue. Because of condi-tions in Lower Canada, the struggle over patronage "s'inscrivent à ce niveau global—c'est-à-dire à un niveau qui assume et intè-gre d'un coup tous les paliers d'intérêt et de conflit . . . . La confiner au niveau purement politique ou la crise d'un groupe social particulier, c'est la tronquer. Craig d'ailleurs l'a bien compris." At the end of their book the authors hope that their study will encourage more extended anal-ysis on similar lines of Canadian institu-tions in the nineteenth century—"c'est cette porte que nous avons voulu entr'-ouvrir." The next three chapters of this present work describe the new political landscape visible through that open door.

NOTES TO CHAPTER 2

1. Helen Taft Manning, "The Colonial Policy of the Whig Ministers 1830-1837," *CHR* 33 (1952):205-14.

2. Kennedy, *Documents on the Canadian Constitution,* pp. 356-57. In England, the Duke of Wellington, still fighting in the ultra-Tory cause, was "violently opposed" to this legislation. For the view of Canadian Tories on this act and British policies since 1830, see J.B. Robinson to Sir George Arthur, London, 31 August 1839 in *The Arthur Papers,* 2, p. 229. The course of the struggle over getting and spending of revenue is described in D.G. Creighton, "The Struggle for Financial Control 1818-1831," pp. 120-44.

3. Sir George Arthur to Glenelg, Toronto, 24 June 1839, *The Arthur Papers,* 1, p. 178.

4. Arthur to Sir John Macdonald, Toronto, 27 February 1839, ibid., pp. 66-67.

5. John Strachan to Henry Phillpots, Bishop of Exeter, 11 May 1845, in J.L.H. Henderson, *John Strachan: Documents and Opinions* (Toronto, 1969), 176.

6. J.C. Dent, *The Last Forty Years: The Union of 1841 to Confederation* (Toronto, 1881), pp. 141, 171-73. Page references are to the modern edition edited by Donald Swainson (Toronto, 1972).

7. Louis P. Turcotte, *Le Canada sous l'Union 1841-1867, Quebec, 1871-72,* 2, p. 5.

8. H.J. Hanham, ed., *The Nineteenth Century Constitution,* (Cambridge, 1969), p. 13 This constitutional understanding which seemed so clear-cut and well-known by the 1840's was, of course, not so generally understood in the 1790's.

9. Manning, "Colonial Policy 1830-1837," p. 352; Pacquet and Wallot, *Patronage et Pouvoir 1794-1812,* pp. 58-59.

10. Dent, *The Last Forty Years,* pp. 53, 56; Ouellet, *Histoire Economique et Sociale,* pp. 196-212; Ouellet, "Le Nationalisme Canadien-Francais: De ses Origines a l'insurrection de 1837," *CHR,* 45 (1964): 277-92. Merritt was a Reform member of the assembly from 1832 to 1860.

11. Poulett Thomson to Lord John Russell, Toronto, 15 December 1839, *The Arthur Papers,* 2, pp. 346-49.

12. Ibid., pp. 346-47. Thomson's critique of past failures was exaggerated. The attorney general was a member of the House after 1820 and so was the solicitor general

after 1830. Executive policy could be effectively implemented if energetic and resourceful leaders like J.B. Robinson put their minds to it. Robinson, for example, used the device of joint assembly-council committees to implement public works and associated large scale borrowing. See R.L. Fraser, "Gentry Society and Economy in Upper Canada 1812-1840," (Ph.D. diss. Toronto, 1979), pp. 163-65. Still, as a contrast of Canadian with British developments, Thomson's critique hit the nail on the head.

13. Lucas, ed., *The Durham Report,* 2, pp. 79-81; Peter Burroughs, *The Colonial Reformers 1830-1849,* pp. 140-41.

14. Turcotte, *Le Canada sous l'Union,* 1, pp. 19-20.

15. Thomson to Arthur, Toronto, December 1839; Arthur to Colborne, Toronto, 9 May 1839, *The Arthur Papers,* 2, pp. 144, 338.

16. Elgin to Grey, Toronto, 6 June 1850 and 1 November 1850; Grey to Elgin, London, 25 November 1850, *Elgin-Grey Papers* (Ottawa, 1937), 2, pp. 683-86, 733, 735.

17. *Spectator,* 19 February 1848, quoted in Burroughs, *The Colonial Reformers 1830-1849,* p. 171. "By that habit which is second nature they are demagogues rather than politicians."

18. Ouellet, *Histoire Economique et Sociale,* pp. 95-97, 274-78.

19. J.B. Robinson to Arthur, London, 23 February 1839, *The Arthur Papers,* 2, p. 62.

20. Robinson to Arthur, Paris, 14 September 1839, ibid., 2, p. 248.

21. Dent, *The Last Forty Years,* p. 82.

22. John Macaulay to Arthur, 15 September 1839, *The Arthur Papers,* 2, p. 263.

23. Elgin to Grey, Montreal, 27 August 1849, *Elgin-Grey Papers,* 2, p. 452.

24. The standard account is Aileen Dunham, *Political Unrest in Upper Canada 1815-1836.* See too, Henderson, *John Strachan: Documents and Opinions* (Toronto, 1969), pp. 86-115 and Craig, *Upper Canada,* pp. 165-225. On settlement of the church and university issues in 1854, see J.M.S. Careless, *The Union of the Canadas 1841-1867* (Toronto, 1967), pp. 194-195. It should be remembered (as part of a reasonable defence of the Tory position) that in 1842 the Anglicans were the single largest denomination in Upper Canada.

25. Colin Read, *The Rising in Western Upper Canada 1837-1838* (Toronto, 1982); F. Landon, *Western Ontario and the American Frontier* (Toronto, 1941); Careless, *Union of the Canadas*, p. 196.

26. Manning, "Colonial Policy 1830-1837," pp. 352-53. "The crux of the problem in the Canadas was to strengthen the position of the governor in his dealings with the people's representatives just as the strengthening of the position of the Crown in its dealings with Parliament had been the main concern of Stuarts and Hanoverians after 1688."

27. In 1839, Colborne suggested setting up a Court of Impeachment to provide for the trial of officials accused of negligent administration. Colborne to Arthur, Montreal, 27 August 1839, *The Arthur Papers* 2, p. 222. See too the interesting work of Carol Wilton-Siegel, "Administrative Reform: A Tory Alternative to Responsible Government," Paper read at CHA Annual Meeting, Vancouver, 1983.

28. Dent, *The Last Forty Years,* pp. 36-60; Elgin to Grey, Toronto, 17 December 1850, *Elgin-Grey Papers,* 2, p. 50; Careless, *Union of the Canadas*, pp. 37-57.

29. Lucas, *The Durham Report,* 2, pp. 101-3, 277-80; Burroughs, *Colonial Reformers 1830-1849,* pp. 95-96, 145-46.

30. Lucas, *The Durham Report,* 2, pp. 101-3. Ged Martin, *The Durham Report* (Cambridge, 1972) points out for the benefit of those scholars who portrayed Durham as an innovative thinker that his concept of strong crown authority was "backward looking."

31. Baldwin to Peter Perry, 16 March 1836, *The Arthur Papers,* 1, p. 7; Dent, *The Last Forty Years,* p. 90.

32. Careless, *Union of the Canadas*, pp. 38-41; Dent, *The Last Forty Years,* pp. 53-59, 113-15, 135, 256. To the very end of his career, Alan McNab, the Tory chief, looked to the governor to sustain him in office against the increasing claims of the young Macdonald.

33. Careless, *Union of the Canadas*, pp. 5-7.

34. Edward Gibbon Wakefield, *A View of Sir Charles Metcalfe's Government of Canada* (London, 1844), quoted in Burroughs, *Colonial Reformers 1830-1849,* p. 167.

35. Norman Gash, *Aristocracy and the People. Britain 1815-1865,* pp. 159-60.

36. Ibid., p. 220; Norman Gash, *Reaction and Reconstruction in English Politics 1832-1852* (Oxford, 1965).

37. Dent, *The Last Forty Years,* pp. 53-59, 115, 132-33, 138; Careless, *Union of the Canadas,* pp. 55-57.

38. Arthur to H.J. Boulton, Toronto, 6 March 1840, *The Arthur Papers,* 2, p. 452.

39. Thomson to Russell, 15 December 1839, ibid., 2, pp. 351-52.

40. Careless, *Union of the Canadas,* pp. 79-83.

41. *Colonial Gazette,* 21 September 1844, in Burroughs, *Colonial Reformers 1830-1849,* p. 168.

42. George Metcalfe, "William Henry Draper," in J.M.S. Careless, ed., *Pre-Confederation Premiers: Ontario Government Leaders 1841-1867* (Toronto, 1980), p. 64; J.M.S. Careless, "Robert Baldwin," ibid., p. 129.

43. Careless, *Union of the Canadas,* pp. 83-84; Dent, *The Last Forty Years,* pp. 115, 132-33, 138; Turcotte, *Le Canada sous l'Union,* pp. 202, 221.

44. Egerton Ryerson, *The Story of My Life* (Toronto, 1884), 312-13. Ryerson viewed the struggle as centred on "the then unsettled question of responsible government as against the prerogative."

45. A.D. Harvey, *Britain in the Early Nineteenth Century,* (New York, 1978), p. 2.

46. Turcotte, *Le Canada sous l'Union,* p. 157.

47. Careless, *Union of the Canadas,* pp. 85-86.

48. *Colonial Gazette,* 21 September 1844, in Burroughs, *Colonial Reformers 1830-1849,* p. 168.

49. Careless, *Union of the Canadas,* p. 79.

50. Ibid., p. 83.

51. Ibid., p. 80; Dent, *The Last Forty Years,* pp. 115, 125.

52. Ryerson, *The Story of My Life,* pp. 312, 320, 323-25.

53. Turcotte, *Le Canada sous l'Union,* p. 199.

54. Ibid., pp. 164, 174-75; Careless, *Union of the Canadas,* p. 83; Monet, *French-Canadian Nationalism 1837-1850,* pp. 167-168, 223.

55. Dent, *The Last Forty Years,* pp. 132-33.

56. *Montreal Gazette,* 6 October 1851, in *Elgin-Grey Papers,* 3, p. 904.

57. Ryerson, *The Story of My Life,* p. 333. This judgment of Ryerson's was based on a précis of a conversation between Metcalfe and LaFontaine given to Ryerson by Metcalfe's civil secretary Higginson. See also Dent, *The Last Forty Years,* p. 177.

58. Robert S.M. Bouchette *Memoires 1805-1840* (Montreal, n.d. [1903?]), pp. 119-20.

59. Careless, *Union of the Canadas*, pp. 41-44; Paul G. Cornell, "The Genesis of Ontario Politics in the Province of Canada 1838-1871," in Zaslow, *Profiles of a Province*, p. 60.

60. Turcotte, *Le Canada sous l'Union*, p. 104n1; Careless, *Union of the Canadas*, p. 41.

61. Craig, *Upper Canada 1784-1841*, pp. 236-37.

62. Monet, *French-Canadian Nationalism 1837-1850*, p. 59; Elgin to Grey, Toronto, 23 March 1850 and Grey to Elgin, London, 21 October 1851, *Elgin-Grey Papers*, 2, pp. 610-11; 3, p. 900; George E. Wilson, *Life of Robert Baldwin* (Toronto, 1933), p. 1, writes of Baldwin's "fine aristocratic sense of honour."

63. Wise, "Upper Canadian Conservative Tradition," in Zaslow, *Profiles of a Province*, pp. 26-29, concluded that patronage-use by the post-1791 elites was "the central fact of provincial politics . . . |and| . . . it was no accident that the reform inspired counciliar crises of 1836 and 1843-44 centered upon the control of crown patronage," As James H. Price summed up to Baldwin, in the Canadas "patronage is power." See Careless, *Union of the Canadas*, p. 76.

64. Turcotte, *Le Canada sous l'Union*, p. 193; Elgin to Grey, Montreal, 14 March 1849, *Elgin-Grey Papers*, 1, p. 308.

65. Elgin to Grey, Montreal, 14 March 1849, *Elgin-Grey Papers*, 1, p. 308.

66. Ryerson, *Story of My Life*, pp. 328-29, 550-51.

67. John Strachan to Robert Gillespie, 2 February 1848, in Henderson, *John Strachan*, p. 178.

68. Joseph Pope, *The Day of Sir John Macdonald* (Toronto, 1920), pp. 27-28; Macpherson, *Life of the Rt. Hon. Sir John A. Macdonald*, p. 190; Peter B. Waite, *Macdonald: His Life and Times* (Toronto, 1975), emphasizes that Macdonald did not like to be ahead of public opinion.

69. Ryerson, *The Story of My Life*, pp. 328-29, 550-51.

70. For example, Elgin to Grey, Montreal, 1847, *Elgin-Grey Papers*, 4, p. 1378; Dufferin to Carnarvon, Ottawa, 13 March 1874, 9 October 1877 and Carnarvon to Dufferin, Newbury, 28 August 1877, in DeKiewiet, *The Dufferin-Carnarvon Correspondence*, 2, p. 365.

71. Harvey, *Britain in the Early Nineteenth Century*, p. 18; J. Vincent, *The Formation of the Liberal Party 1857-1868* (London, 1966), pp. 82-89. O'Gorman, *The Emergence of the British Two-Party System 1760-1832, passim*.

72. Norman Gash, *Politics in the Age of Peel* (Oxford, 1953).

73. Hanham, *Nineteenth Century Constitution*, p. 224.

74. Ibid., pp. 1, 2, 16, 24-30; Robert Blake, *Disraeli* (London, 1967), p. 270.

75. Daniel Owen Maddyn, *Chiefs of Parties: Past and Present* (London, 1859), 1, pp. 10-14.

76. Metcalfe, "William Draper," in Careless, *Pre-Confederation Premiers*, pp. 70, 78; *Elgin-Grey Papers*, 2, pp. 740-42 (Memorandum on State of Political Parties, Quebec, 4 November 1850).

77. Robinson to Arthur, London, 23 February 1839, *The Arthur Papers*, 2, p. 62. "There is in Canada no counteracting influence of an ancient aristocracy, of a great landed interest or even of a wealthy agricultural class." The great complaint of the Tories, ever since 1828, had been that Britain was yielding to democratic pressures in Canada. Britain, explained C.A. Hagerman was agreeing to make colonial government "more democratic than it is—and that the power of the Crown instead of being strengthened should be relaxed—and that the opinions and wishes of a Provincial House of Assembly is to guide the administration of public affairs. What chance is there of maintaining that control which is essential to the effective government of a Colony if this policy is avowed and pursued." C.A. Hagerman to Arthur, May 1839, *The Arthur Papers*, 2, p. 142.

78. Careless, *Union of the Canadas*, pp. 25, 31-32.

79. *Spectator*, 19 February 1848, in Burroughs, *The Colonial Reformers 1830-1849*, p. 171; Thomson to Russell, Toronto, 15 December 1839, *The Arthur Papers*, 2, pp. 345-64; Dent, *The Last Forty Years*, p. 139.

80. Elgin to Grey, Montreal, 30 April 1849, *Elgin-Grey Papers*, 4, p. 1460.

81. Dufferin to Carnarvon, Ottawa, 10 October 1874, *Dufferin-Carnarvon Correspondence*, p. 108.

82. Joseph Pope, *Day of Sir John Macdonald* (Toronto, 1920), p. 176; Peter B. Waite, *Canada 1874-1896: Arduous Destiny* (Toronto, 1964), pp. 221-25.

83. Donald Creighton, *John A. Macdonald: The Old Chieftain* (Toronto, 1955), pp. 219-24, 232-34.
84. Careless, *Union of the Canadas.* p. 116.
85. Norman Ward, "Responsible Government: an Introduction," *Journal of Canadian Studies (JCS).* 14 (1979): 3; Macdonald to A. Watts, 26 February 1880, Joseph Pope, ed., *Correspondence of Sir John Macdonald* (Toronto, 1921), pp. 271-72.

NOTES TO CHAPTER 3

1. W.L. Morton, *The Critical Years,* p. 11.
2. Plumb, *The Growth of Political Stability 1675-1725.* p. 168; Speck, *Stability and Strife 1714-1760.* p. 143-166.
3. Peter B. Waite, *The Life and Times of Confederation 1864-1867* (Toronto, 1962), pp. 65-66.
4. Elgin to Grey, Toronto, 15 July 1850, *Elgin-Grey Papers,* 2, p. 697.
5. Macdonald to Ogle Gowan, 30 April 1847, in Christopher Armstrong, "The Macdonald-Gowan Letters," *Ontario History.* 63 (1971). On Macdonald's role in settling the old contentious issues that had disturbed Canadian politics since 1800, see Creighton, *John A. Macdonald: The Young Politician.* pp. 208-15.
6. G. Mercer Adam, *Canada's Patriot Statesman: The Life and Career of the Rt. Hon. John A. Macdonald* (Toronto, 1891), p. 69; George Parkin, *Sir John A. Macdonald* (Toronto, 1907 |1926|), p. 349.
7. P.G. Cornell, *The Alignment of Political Groups in Canada 1841-1867* (Toronto, 1962); Dent, *The Last Forty Years.* p. 51.
8. Macdonald to Henry C.R. Becher, 5 December 1857 and 14 December 1857 in J.K. Johnson, ed., *The Letters of Sir John A. Macdonald 1836-1857* (Ottawa, 1968), pp. 466, 472.
9. Careless, *Union of the Canadas.* pp. 76-77.
10. Macdonald to Brown Chamberlin, 21 January 1856, quoted in ibid., p. 189.
11. William Ormsby, "Francis Hincks," in Careless, *Pre-Confederation Premiers.* p. 157.
12. Dent, *The Last Forty Years.* p. 215, wrote of the Grits that they "embody the whole difference between a republican form of Government and the limited monarchy of Great Britain." In 1850, Grey warned Elgin that "looking forward, it seems to me that this (the Grit party) is much the most dangerous party in Canada." Grey to Elgin, London, 12 April 1850, *The Elgin-Grey Papers.* 2, p. 605. See too Careless, *Pre-Confederation Premiers.* pp. 139, 160, and Careless, *Brown of The Globe* (Toronto, 1959), 1, p. 311.
13. Elwood Jones, "Ephemeral Compromise: The Great Reform Convention Re-visited," *JCS.* 3 (1968):21-22.
14. Elgin to Grey, Monklands, 24 February 1847; Elgin to Grey, Montreal, 27 March 1847; Elgin to Grey, Toronto, 14 June 1851; Elgin to Grey, 22 November 1850, in *Elgin-Grey Papers,* 1, pp. 14-20, 2, pp. 746, 827.
15. Creighton, *John A. Macdonald: The Young Politician.* p. 342.
16. W.L. Morton, *The Critical Years: 1857-1873,* pp. 68, 72, 209; R.G. Trotter, "British Finance and Confederation," CHA *Report* (1927). George Brown noted that as soon as the Confederation resolutions were published in the London papers "the immediate effect of the scheme was such on the public mind that our 5%'s rose from 75 to 92."
17. Macdonald to S.I. Lynn, 10 April 1866 in Pope, *Correspondence of Sir John Macdonald,* pp. 31-32.
18. Creighton, *John A. Macdonald: The Old Chieftain.* pp. 36-37.
19. Dent, *The Last Forty Years,* p. 291.
20. Cornell, *The Alignment of Political Groups 1844-1867,* p. 85.
21. Keith Johnson, ed., *Affectionately Yours: The Letters of John A. Macdonald and his Family* (Toronto, 1969), pp. 160-61.
22. Macdonald to Ogle Gowan, 3 November 1847, in Armstrong, "The Macdonald-Gowan Letters," pp. 1-14.
23. Ibid., pp. 6, 13.
24. Norman Ward, "Responsible Government: an Introduction," *JCS* 14 (1979):3.
25. Peter G. Richards, *Patronage in British Government* (London, 1963), pp. 30, 37, 41, 58, 60-61; Richard Hofstadter, *The Idea of a Party System: the Rise of Legitimate Opposition in the United States 1780-1840* (Berkeley, 1969), pp. 217, 262-63.

26. *The Bystander,* April 1883, p. 88.
27. Macdonald to Dufferin, 9 October 1873, in Joseph Pope, *Memoirs of Sir John Macdonald* (Toronto, 1921), p. 553.
28. Macdonald to Carnarvon, 14 April 1870, in Pope, *Correspondence of Sir John A. Macdonald,* pp. 132-33.
29. List of QCs in Toronto, n.d. [Winter 1889-90], Macdonald Papers, vol. 24, Public Archives of Canada (PAC).
30. J.K. Johnson, ed., *The Letters of Sir John A. Macdonald 1836-1857* (Ottawa, 1969), p. xx.
31. Joseph Pope, *The Day of Sir John Macdonald* (Toronto, 1920), pp. 149-51. This characterization of Campbell is even more arresting when it is understood just what Campbell *did* do for the party. See Donald Swainson, "Alexander Campbell: General Manager of the Conservative Party (Eastern Ontario Section)," *Historic Kingston* 17 (1969).
32. J.E. Collins, *Life and Times of the Rt. Hon. John A. Macdonald* (Toronto, 1883), p. 69.
33. Henry Taylor, *The Statesman* (London, 1832), quoted in Richards, *Patronage in British Government,* p. 37.
34. Pamela Cornell, "Collecting Yesterday," in *Graduate The University of Toronto Alumnae Magazine,* 10 (1983):17-19. I am grateful to Professor Keith Johnson for bringing this item to my attention. But it must be pointed out that Wilson had a personal grievance against Macdonald because Wilson had been offered, in 1888, only a Knight Bachelor honour rather than the KCMG which Wilson believed he deserved as the eminent holder of such an illustrious position as president of the University of Toronto. See Wilson to Macdonald, Toronto, 2 June 1888, in Pope, *Correspondence of Sir John A. Macdonald,* pp. 411-12.
35. *The Bystander,* April 1883, p. 90. But shortly after Macdonald's death Lady Aberdeen noted that "it is supposed that he just took for himself many of the large sums of money sent privately for electioneering purposes." John Saywell, ed., *The Canadian Journal of Lady Aberdeen* (Toronto, 1960), p. 165. But even allowing for the differences in their times, Macdonald fell far short of Walpole when it came to making personal use of office.
36. Macdonald to M.C. Cameron, 3 January

1872, in Pope *Correspondence of Sir John Macdonald,* p. 161; Macdonald to John Carling, 23 December 1871, in Pope, *Memoirs of Sir John A. Macdonald,* pp. 501-3. See Creighton, *John A. Macdonald: The Old Chieftain,* p. 126, and Stewart, "Macdonald's Greatest Triumph," *CHR,* 63 (1982): 23-24.
37. Stewart, "Macdonald's Greatest Triumph," pp. 3-27.
38. *The Bystander,* April 1883, p. 266.
39. Creighton, *John A. Macdonald: The Old Chieftain,* p. 426; Norman Ward, *The Canadian House of Commons* (Toronto: University of Toronto Press, 1963), viii, pp. 191-94.
40. Macdonald to Charles Tupper, 27 July 1885, quoted in Creighton, *John A. Macdonald: The Old Chieftain,* p. 427.
41. Stewart, "Macdonald's Greatest Triumph," pp. 26-27.
42. Johnson, "Macdonald," in Careless, *Pre-Confederation Premiers,* p. 209.
43. Dent, *The Last Forty Years,* p. 158.
44. Jones, *Patronage in British Government,* pp. 30, 37, 41.
45. Dufferin to Carnarvon, Ottawa, 18 March 1874, *Dufferin-Carnarvon Correspondence,* pp. 13-14.
46. Dale C. Thomson, *Alexander Mackenzie: Clear Grit* (Toronto, 1960), p. 77; Careless, *Pre-Confederation Premiers,* pp. 10-11; Jones, *Patronage in British Government,* pp. 60-61 writes that "job filling troubled the Liberal conscience in a way unknown to the Tory mind."
47. J.D. Livermore, "The Personal Agonies of Edward Blake, " *CHR,* 56 (1975):51.
48. Waite, *Canada 1874-1896,* pp. 13-92.
49. Donald Swainson, ed., *Oliver Mowat's Ontario* (Toronto, 1972), pp. 1-7, and Bruce W. Hodgins, "Disagreement at the Commencement," ibid., pp. 52-68; Christopher Armstrong, "The Mowat Heritage in Federal-Provincial Relations," ibid., pp. 93-118; Christopher Armstrong, *The Politics of Federalism, Ontario's Relations with the Federal Government 1867-1942* (Toronto, 1981), pp. 8-32.
50. Macdonald to John Carling, 23 December 1871, in Pope. *Memoirs of Sir John Macdonald,* pp. 501-3.
51. Hodgins, "Disagreement at the Commencement: Divergent Ontarian Views of Confederation 1867-1871," in Swainson, *Oliver Mowat's Ontario,* pp. 52-68 is a fine analysis of Mowat's views and tactics.

52. W.L. Russell and Adam Hudspeth to Macdonald, Lindsay, 16 February 1880, Private, Macdonald Papers, vol. 25, 1, PAC. The way in which appointments were distributed in a systematic manner to local parties can be seen from a case that came to light in 1891 concerning appointments and contracts connected with the Murray Canal. In discussing the distribution of posts, Macdonald asked Mackenzie Bowell whether the riding of East Northumberland was "to have the whole patronage of the Murray Canal?" Mackenzie Bowell replied: "Certainly not. I told him |Cochrane, the Conservative MP for East Northumberland| over a year ago that the canal was not an East Northumberland one, but of Dominion character, and that West Hastings and Prince Edward must be considered in all appointments." See Report of Select Committee to Inquire into Charges against the Member for East Northumberland, *Canada. House of Commons. Journals.* 25 (1891), 11, Appendix 4, pp. xix-xx.

53. Livermore, "Personal Agonies of Edward Blake," p. 51.

54. Marcel Hamelin, ed., *Les Mémoires du Senateur Raoul Dandurand* (Quebec, 1967), pp. 25, 47-56.

55. Roy Choquette to Wilfrid Laurier, Ottawa, 12 September 1896, Personelle, Laurier Papers, vol. 833, PAC; H.G. Carroll to Wilfrid Laurier, Quebec, 29 December 1896 and Memo in Reply (n.d.), ibid., vol. 833; Deputy Postmaster-General to Laurier, Ottawa, 23 November 1906, ibid., vol. 925; Paul Stevens, "Wilfrid Laurier Politician," in Marcel Hamelin, ed., *Political Ideas of the Prime Ministers* (Ottawa, 1969), pp. 80-82; Stewart, "Political Patronage under Macdonald and Laurier," *American Review of Canadian Studies*, 10, (1980): 9-12; H. Blair Neatby, *Laurier and a Liberal Quebec* (Toronto, 1973), pp. 122-49.

56. George Reid to James Sutherland, London, 4 May 1900, Laurier Papers, vol. 873, PAC.

57. R.C. Brown and Ramsay Cook, *A Nation Transformed: Canada 1896-1920* (Toronto, 1974), p. 150; D.G. Creighton, *Canada's First Century* (Toronto, 1970), pp. 99-100.

58. Quoted in Paul Stevens, "Laurier and the Liberal Party in Quebec 1887-1911,"

Ph.D. diss., University of Toronto, 1966, pp. 252-53. Brown and Cook, *Canada 1896-1921.* pp. 165-167 gives a cogent summary of all the issues involved in the militia question at this time.

59. Commission to Inquire into the Present State and Probable Requirements of the Civil Service (1868-70), First and Second Reports in *Canada, House of Commons, Sessional Papers,* no. 19 (1869), Third Report in ibid., no. 64 (1870); Royal Commission to Inquire into the Organization of the Civil Service Commission (1880-81), First Report in ibid., no. 113 (1880-81), Second Report in ibid., no. 32 (1882); Royal Commission to Inquire into the Present State of the Civil Service at Ottawa (1891-92), Report in ibid., no. 16C (1892); Report of the Civil Service Commission (1907-8), ibid., no. 29A (1907-8); Commission to Inquire into the Public Service (1911-12), ibid., no. 57 (1913). Select Committee to Inquire into the Present Condition of the Civil Service, *Canada, House of Commons Journals* 2 (1877): Appendix 7. See following notes for specific references.

60. W.L. Morton, "The Cabinet of 1867," in F.W. Gibson, ed., *Cabinet Formation and Bicultural Relations* (Ottawa, 1970), p. 2.

61. Waite, *Canada 1874-1896,* p. 96.

62. Report of Select Committee to Inquire into the Present Condition of the Civil Service, *Canada, House of Commons, Journals,* 11, (1877): Appendix 7, pp. 3-5.

63. Report of the Civil Service Commission, *Canada, House of Commons, Sessional Papers* 42 (1907-8) 15 |hereafter Civil Service Commission| (1907-8), pp. 13-15.

64. R. MacGregor Dawson, "The Canadian Civil Service," *Canadian Journal of Economics and Political Science* 11 (1936).

65. Notes on Civil Service Reform by William LeSueur, *Canada, House of Commons. Journals,* 11 (1877): Appendix 7, p. 106.

66. Civil Service Commission (1907-8), pp. 9, 13-15.

67. Ibid., pp. 176, 205.

68. Report of an Investigation into the Department of Marine and Fisheries, *Canada, House of Commons, Sessional Papers* 42 (1909): 17, no. 38, pp. 10, 41-43.

69. Ibid.

70. See discussion in Stewart, "Macdonald's Greatest Triumph," p. 25n91.

71. John Small to Macdonald, Toronto, 5 April 1887, Confidential, Macdonald Papers, vol. 24, PAC.

72. A.M. Boswell to Macdonald, Toronto, 7 July 1887, Macdonald Papers, vol. 27 II, PAC. Boswell wrote of N.L. Stewart of Hamilton (whom he was recommending for a judgeship), that he was "an out and out Conservative and as steady as a rock. At one time he was not a cold water man but now he is all right." A Conservative MP recommending a barrister for a QC told Macdonald that the man had "been true to the party in season and out." See W. Tisdale to Macdonald, Ottawa, 19 June 1887, Macdonald Papers, vol. 24, PAC. It was exactly this kind of dedicated party service in good and bad times that Macdonald steadily rewarded.

73. John Barwick to Macdonald, Woodstock, 10 February, 1879, Macdonald Papers, vol. 25I, PAC.

74. Robert Birmingham to Macdonald, Toronto, 10 October 1889, Macdonald Papers, vol. 24, PAC.

75. Alexander Finkle to Macdonald, Woodstock, 1 February 1879, Macdonald Papers, vol. 25I, PAC.

76. A.M. Francis to Macdonald, Woodstock, 16 April 1879, John Barwick to Macdonald, Woodstock, 10 February 1879, Macdonald Papers, vol. 25I, PAC.

77. J.W. Nesbitt to Macdonald, 21 April 1879, ibid.

78. A. McGloughlin to Macdonald, Woodstock, 21 April 1879, ibid.

79. John Carling to Macdonald, London, 22 April 1879, ibid.

80. N.O. Coté, *Political Appointments, Parliaments and the Judicial Bench in Canada 1867-1895* (Ottawa, 1896), p. 328.

81. W.L. Payne to Macdonald, Ottawa, 19 September 1881, Macdonald Papers, vol. 25II, PAC.

82. J.R. Ketcheson to Macdonald, Madoc. 1 October 1881, ibid.

83. Alexander Robertson to Macdonald, Belleville, 1 October 1881, Private, ibid.

84. Coté, *Political Appointments*, p. 321.

85. B.L. Doyle to Frank Smith, Goderich, 28 November 1879, Private, Macdonald Papers, vol. 25II, PAC.

86. Frank Smith to Macdonald, 1 December 1879, ibid.

87. Bishop of Hamilton to Macdonald, Hamilton, 15 October 1880, ibid.

88. Reverend Fathers George R. North and James Murphy to Macdonald, Private, 25 October 1880 and 2 December 1880, ibid.

89. Frederick W. Johnston to Macdonald, Goderich, 5 March 1881 and 13 December 1881, Private, ibid.; N.M. Reay to Macdonald, Clinton, 29 April 1881 and William Campbell to Macdonald, Goderich, 5 May 1881, Private, ibid.

90. Coté, *Political Appointments*, p. 322.

91. Ward, *Canadian House of Commons*, pp. vii-viii.

92. Ibid., pp. 189-90. Ward saw no greater virtue on the Liberal side. Reform of the electoral system and the reduction of the worst of partisan abuse did not come through the initiatives of either party but because of the influence of public opinion. These observations by Ward confirm in yet another way that the political system had been formed by values and attitudes of the 1840's. See Ward, "Electoral Corruption and Controverted Elections," *CJEPS*, 15 (1949): pp. 84-85.

93. R.M. Dawson, "The Gerrymander of 1882," *CJEPS* 1 (1934): pp. 199-200, 204, 206.

94. Stewart, "Macdonald's Greatest Triumph," p. 27.

95. This pattern was also already well-established during the Union period and even in the Canadas between 1791 and 1840 with their canal schemes. During Macdonald's first two decades in politics the railway mania was at its height. Long before Confederation, Canadian governments had acquired the habit of large expenditure and deep involvement with transportation and other public works. Dent, *The Last Forty Years*, p. 237; Turcotte, *Le Canada sous l'Union*, 2, pp. 147, 155, 195; Careless, *Union of the Canadas*, p. 145. J. Henry Ince, a Toronto lawyer, wrote to Macdonald in 1880: "there are new counties being erected and changes continually taking place which throw into the hands of our party a large amount of patronage," J. Henry Ince to Macdonald, Toronto, 5 July 1880, Macdonald Papers, vol. 25I., PAC.

96. Waite, *Canada 1874-1896* pp. 74-78, 96, provides a summary of conventional wisdom on this subject of Canadian economic growth.

97. M.C. Urquhart and K.A.H. Buckley, eds.,

Historical Statistics of Canada (Toronto, 1965), p. 463, Series Q 1-11; S.D. Clark, "The Canadian Manufacturers Association," *CJEPS* 4 (1938): 506-8; R.T. Naylor, *The History of Canadian Business 1867-1914*, 2 vols. (Toronto, 1975), pp. 276-84 argues that Canadian industrial development was stultified during these years. Dufferin informed Carnarvon that "in spite of their high-sounding names the Canadian Boards of Trade do not enjoy any great consideration." Manufacturers, he added, formed "but a small proportion of the population of Canada." Dufferin to Carnarvon, Ottawa, 2 October 1874 and Toronto, 3 September 1874, in *Dufferin-Carnarvon Correspondence*, p. 77.

98. Waite, *Canada 1874-1896* pp. 74-78.
99. Proceedings and Report of Special Committee to Consider the Unsatisfactory Character of the Movement of the Population Especially in the Older Provinces of the Dominion as shown in the last Census. *Canada, Senate, Journals* 40 (1911-12); Brown and Cook *Canada 1896-1921*, p. 186.
100. Michael Bliss, *A Living Profit. Studies in the Social History of Canadian Business* (Toronto, 1974), pp. 114-15, quoting *Monetary Times* 21 June 1896; *Journal of Commerce* 4 November 1898, Byron Walker to G.P. Little, 10 October 1907.
101. H.V. Nelles, *The Politics of Development* (Toronto, 1974), pp. 383-84, 491.
102. Christopher Armstrong, *The Politics of Federalism* (Toronto, 1981), pp. 5, 233.
103. Nelles, *Politics of Development* p. 494.
104. Armstrong, *Politics of Federalism*, p. 233.
105. Civil Service Commission (1907-8), pp. 14-17.
106. Commission to Inquire into the Public Service (1911-12), *Canada, House of Commons, Sessional Papers* no. 57 (1913): 1213.
107. Ward, *Canadian House of Commons*, pp. 98-101, 103, 146. Christopher Robinson told Macdonald in 1878 that the "three inducements" which made judgeships attractive were "dignity—ease—and the prospect of a Pension." Robinson to Macdonald, Toronto, 28 December 1878, Macdonald Papers, vol. 251, PAC.
108. Jacques Monet, "Les Idées politiques de Baldwin and LaFontaine," in Marcel Hamelin, *The Political Ideas of the Prime*

Ministers, pp. 16-17. See too Charles Langelier, *Souvenirs Politiques* (Quebec, 1912), pp. 25-26.
109. J.C. Falardeau, "Evolution des structures sociales et des élites au Canada Francais," in Guy Sylvestre, ed., *Structures Sociales du Canada Francais* (Quebec, 1960), pp. 10-11.
110. Ibid., p. 11.
111. Jean-Charles Bonenfant, "L'évolution du statut de l'homme politique Canadien-Francais," in Fernand Dumont et Jean-Paul Montmigny, ed., *Le Pouvoir dans la Societé Canadien Francais* (Quebec, 1966), pp. 117-18.
112. Clark, *The Developing Political Community*, 234, 237.
113. J.M. Beck, *Joseph Howe: The Briton Becomes Canadian, 1848-1873* (Kingston and Montreal, 1983), pp. 264-65, 256-57, 272-73, 278; Peter B. Waite, "Becoming Canadians: Ottawa's Relations with Maritimers in the First and Twenty-first Years of Confederation" (Paper read at CHA Annual Meeting, Vancouver, 1983), draws attention once again to the place of patronage in the relationship.
114. Beck, *Joseph Howe*, 2, p. 16.
115. Ibid., p. 15.
116. André Siegfried, *The Race Question in Canada* (Paris, 1907), p. 117. Page references are to the edition edited by F.H. Underhill (Toronto, 1966).
117. Ibid., p. 114.
118. A.B. McKillop, ed., *A Critical Spirit: The Thought of William Dawson LeSueur* (Toronto, 1977); Robert Laird Borden, *Memoirs* (Toronto, 1938), pp. 130, 191-92, 197-98, 324-25.
119. Joseph LaPalombara, ed., *Bureaucracy and Political Development* (Princeton, 1963), p. 11. In his assessment of the literature on political development, La Palombara concluded that "corruption or its functional equivalent may be critically important to the developing nation." The "petite peu de graise" phrase was made by a witness before Judge Cassels during the inquiry into the Department of Marine and Fisheries. He was justifying the patronage system in general in the department and in particular the 5 per cent surcharge added to all contracts to make the system work smoothly. Report of Investigation into the Department of Marine and Fisheries, *Canada,*

House of Commons, Sessional Papers 42
(1909): 17, no. 38, pp. 21, 27-28. In 1884,
Mr. Justice Armour was quoted in *The
Week* (11 December 1884) as saying "Is

not bribery the corner-stone of Party
Government." See Ward, *Canadian House
of Commons*, p. 245.

NOTES TO CHAPTER 4

1. Brown and Cook, *Canada 1896-1921* is the
starting point for understanding the transition to modern politics.
2. J.L. Granatstein, *A Man of Influence, Norman A. Robertson and Canadian State-
craft* (Ottawa, 1981). J.E. Hodgetts, et al.,
*The Biography of an Institution: The Civil
Service Commission of Canada 1908-1967*
(Montreal, 1967) describes the modern
system and its methods of quality control.
3. Wise, "The Upper Canadian Conservative Tradition," in Zaslow, *Profiles of a
Province*, pp. 26-29.
4. G.R. Stevens, *History of the Canadian
National Railways* (Toronto, 1973), Chapter 5.
5. Civil Service Commission Report (1907-
8), p. 37.
6. Stewart, "Macdonald's Greatest Triumph,"
pp. 3-33.
7. J. Farnelly to Macdonald, Belleville, 6
October 1881, Macdonald Papers, vol.
25II, PAC. See too James Young, *Public
Men and Public Life in Canada* (Toronto,
1902), p. 341.
8. Hugh J. Macdonald to Macdonald, 7 January 1890, in Johnson, *The Letters of Sir
John A. Macdonald and his Family* pp.
188-89; Waite, *Canada 1874-1896*, p. 229.
9. Richards, *Patronage in British Government*, pp. 58-61.
10. Sullivan Report on the State of the Province, June 1838, *Arthur Papers*, 1, p. 164.
11. J.E. Hodgetts, *The Provincial Governments as Employers* (Toronto, 1979), describes the culmination of these trends.
12. Laurier to Hugh Falcolner, Ottawa, 15
January 1908, Private, Laurier Papers, vol.

950, PAC. See too Report of Investigation
into the Department of Marine and Fisheries, *Canada, House of Commons, Sessional Papers* 42 (1909): 17, no. 38, pp. 10,
41, 42-44.
13. Civil Service Commission Report 1907-8,
p. 89.
14. William LeSueur, "Party Politics," *Canadian Monthly and National Review*, 11
(November 1872): 447-55, quoted in Mc-
Killop, ed., *A Critical Spirit*, p. 184.
15. Dufferin to Carnarvon, Ottawa, 10 October 1874, *Dufferin-Carnarvon Correspondence*, p. 108; Siegfried, *The Race Question in Canada*, p. 117.
16. Hans Muller, *Canada: Past, Present and
Future* (Montreal, 1880), p. 7.
17. Robert A. MacKay, *The Unreformed Senate of Canada* (Toronto, 1963), describes
the workings of the system. The Macdonald and Laurier papers at the Public
Archives show how party considerations
reigned supreme when it came to appointing senators.
18. Notes on Civil Service Reform by William
LeSueur, Report of the Select Committee
on Present Conditions in the Civil Service,
Canada, House of Commons, Journals 11
(1877): Appendix 7, p. 106.
19. Kenneth D. McRae, *Consociational Democracy: Political Accommodation in
Segmented Societies* (Toronto, 1974), pp.
250, 254, 259-61.
20. Brown and Cook, *Canada 1896-1921*, pp.
164-65.
21. J. Peter Meekison, *Canadian Federalism*
(Toronto, 1968), p. 8.
22. Dent, *The Last Forty Years*, p. 158.

BIBLIOGRAPHY

A complete bibliography of items bearing on this topic would merely be a rearranged version of the bibliographies listed in Hilda Neatby, *Quebec: The Revolutionary Age 1760-1791* (Toronto, 1966), Fernand Ouellet, *Histoire Economique et Sociale du Québec 1760-1850* (Montreal, 1966), Gerald M. Craig, *Upper Canada: The Formative years 1784-1841* (Toronto, 1963), J.M.S. Careless, *The Union of the Canadas: The Growth of Canadian Institutions 1841-1857* (Toronto, 1967), W.L. Morton, *The Critical Years: The Union of British North America 1857-1873* (Toronto, 1964), Peter B. Waite, *Canada 1874-1896: Arduous Destiny* (Toronto, 1971) and R.C. Brown and Ramsay Cook, *Canada 1896-1921: A Nation Transformed* (Toronto, 1974) along with books and articles on the Anglo-American background since 1688 listed in the bibliographies of such standard works as J.R. Jones, *Country and Court: England 1658-1714* (Cambridge, MA, 1979), W.A. Speck, *Stability and Strife: England 1714-1760* (London, 1977), Norman Gash, *Aristocracy and the People: Britain 1815-1865* (Cambridge, MA, 1979), Bernard Bailyn, *The Origins of American Politics* (New York, 1968), Jack P. Greene, *The Quest for Power: The Lower Houses of Assembly in the Southern Royal Colonies 1689-1776* (Chapel Hill, 1963) and in that excellent comparative analysis of John M. Murrin, "The Great Inversion, or Court versus Country: a Comparison of the Revolution Settlements in England (1688-1721) and America (1776-1816)," in J.G.A. Pocock, ed., *Three British Revolutions 1641, 1688, 1776* (Princeton, 1980), pp. 368-453. Rather than compile a lengthy bibliography covering all this ground, I list here only these items that are cited in the notes or which were of direct use in preparing the case presented in the essay.

I. PRIMARY SOURCES

A. *Manuscript Papers at the Public Archives of Canada.*

Mackenzie Bowell Papers, MG26E
  vol. 77A Patronage Letterbook

Alexander Campbell Papers, MG27I, C2
J.A. Chapleau Papers, MG27I, C3
Alphonse Désjardins Papers, MG27I, E22
Wilfrid Laurier Papers, MG26G
    Selected volumes from the Laurier patronage papers: vols. 833, 850, 873,
    891, 900, 925, 950, 975, 1000, 1005, 1007
John A. Macdonald Papers, MG26A
    vol. 2 Applications for Office 1882
    vol. 5 Applications for Office 1882/83
    vol. 9 Revising Officers 1883/85
    vol. 10 Revising Officers 1885
    vol. 11 Revising Officers 1885
    vol. 14 Kingston Patronage
    vols. 15, 16, 17, 19, 22 Senatorships 1878-1891
    vols. 23 QC Appointments 1879/81
    vol. 24 QC Appointments 1886/89
    vol. 25 Judicial Appointments 1878/81
    vol. 26 Judicial Appointments 1882/86
    vol. 27 Judicial Appointments 1887/90
Alexander Smith Papers, MG27II, H14

B. *Canadian Parliamentary Papers*

Commission to inquire into the President State and Probable Requirements of
    the Civil Service (1868-70), 1st and 2nd Reports in *Canada, House of
    Commons, Sessional Papers* 19 (1869), 3rd Report in no. 64 (1870).
Report of Select Committee to Inquire into the Present Condition of the Civil
    Service, *Canada, House of Commons, Journals* 11 (1877): Appendix 7.
Royal Commission to Inquire into the Organization of the Civil Service Com-
    mission (1880-81), 1st Report in *Canada, House of Commons, Sessional
    Papers* 113 (1880-81), 2nd Report in no. 32 (1882).
Royal Commission to Inquire into the Present State of the Civil Service at
    Ottawa (1891-92), *Canada, House of Commons, Sessional Papers.* no. 16C
    (1892).
Report of the Civil Service Commission (1907-8), *Canada, House of Com-
    mons, Sessional Papers* no. 29A (1907-8).
Commission to Inquire into the Public Service (1911-12), *Canada, House of
    Commons, Sessional Papers* no. 57 (1913).
Report of Select Standing Committee on Privileges and Elections re-case of
    F.W. Anglin and Newspaper Patronage, *Canada, House of Commons, Jour-
    nals* 11 (1877): Appendix 8.
First Report of Select Standing Committee on Public Accounts re-payments
    made to J.G. Moylan, ibid., 12 (1878): Appendix 1.
First Report of Standing Committee on Privileges and Elections re-Kent
    County Election, ibid., 22 (1888): Appendix 2.
Report of Select Standing Committee on Privileges and Elections re-charges

against J.C. Rykert, ibid., 24 (1890): Appendix 4.

Report of the Select Committee to Inquire into charges against the Member for East Northumberland, ibid., 25 (1891): vol. 11, Appendix 4.

Report of Select Standing Committee on Privileges and Elections re-charges against Arthur J. Turcotte, Member for Montmorency, ibid., 28 (1894): Appendix ix, p. 3.

Report of Select Standing Committee appointed to supervise the Official Report of the Debates of the House of Commons re-charges against Messrs. Lucien Lasalle, Joseph Bouchard, Peter McLeod and J.B. Vanasse, ibid., 31 (1896): Appendix ix, p. 1.

Report of Select Standing Committee on Privileges and Elections re-West Huron Election, ibid., 34 (1899): Appendix 3.

Report of Select Standing Committee on Public Accounts re-Manitoba Election Frauds, ibid., 34 (1899): Appendix 1.

Proceedings and Report of Special Committee to Consider the Unsatisfactory Character of the Movement of the Population Especially in the Older Provinces of the Dominion as shown by the Last Census, *Canada, Senate, Journals,* 40.

C. *Printed Correspondence*

Armstrong, Frederick. "The Macdonald-Gowan Letters, 1847". *Ontario History.* 63 (1971): 1-14.

Cruikshank, E.A., ed. *The Correspondence of Lieutenant-Governor John Graves Simcoe.* 4 vols. Toronto, 1923.

DeKlewiet, C.W., and F.H. Underhill, eds. *The Dufferin-Carnarvon Correspondence 1874-1878.* Toronto, 1955.

Doughty, A.G., ed. *The Elgin-Grey Papers 1846-1852.* 4 vols. Ottawa, 1937.

Johnson, J.K., ed. *The Letters of Sir John A. Macdonald 1837-1861.* 2 vols. Ottawa, 1968-69.

———, ed. *Affectionately Yours: The Letters of Sir John A. Macdonald and His Family.* Toronto, 1969.

Morton, W.L., ed. *Monck Letters and Journals 1863-1868.* Toronto, 1970.

Pope, Joseph, ed. *Correspondence of Sir John A. Macdonald 1840-1891.* Toronto, 1921.

Sanderson, Charles R., ed. *The Arthur Papers.* 3 vols. Toronto, 1957.

Saywell, John T., ed. *The Canadian Journal of Lady Aberdeen 1893-1898.* Toronto, 1960.

D. *Memoirs, Contemporary Accounts and Reports*

Adam, C. Mercer. *Canada's Patriot Statesman: The Life and Career of the Rt. Hon. Sir John A. Macdonald.* London and Toronto, 1891.

Barthe, Ulric, *Wilfrid Laurier on the Platform 1871-1890.* Quebec, 1890.

Biggar, E.B. *Anecdotal Life of Sir John Macdonald.* Toronto, 1891.

Borden, Henry, ed., *Robert Laird Borden: His Memoirs.* Toronto, 1938.

Bouchette, Robert-S.M. *Mémoires 1805-1840.* Montreal, n.d. (1903).
Burroughs, Peter, ed. *The Colonial Reformers and Canada 1830-1849.* Toronto, 1969.
Cartwright, Richard. *Reminiscences.* Toronto, 1912.
Collins, J.E. *Canada under the Administration of Lord Lorne.* Toronto, 1884.
_____. *Life and Times of the Rt. Hon. Sir John A. Macdonald.* Toronto, 1883.
Dent, J.C. *The Last Forty Years: The Union of 1841 to Confederation.* Toronto, 1972 (1881).
Hamelin, Marcel, ed. *Les Mémoires du senateur Raoul Dandurand.* Quebec, 1957.
Henderson, J.L.H., ed. *John Strachan: Documents and Opinions.* Toronto, 1969.
Langelier, Charles. *Souvenirs Politiques.* Quebec, 1912.
Lucas, Charles, ed. *The Durham Report.* 3 vols. London, 1929.
McKillop, A.B., ed. *A Critical Spirit: The Thought of William Dawson Le-Sueur.* Toronto, 1977.
Macpherson, J. Pennington. *Life of the Rt. Hon. Sir John A. Macdonald.* 2 vols. St. John, NB, 1891.
Maddyn, Daniel Owen. *Chiefs of Parties Past and Present: With Original Anecdotes.* 2 vols. London, 1859.
Muller, Hans. *Canada: Past, Present and Future.* Montreal, 1880.
Ormsby, William. *Crisis in the Canadas 1838-39. The Grey Journals and Letters.* London, 1965.
Pope, Joseph. *Memoirs of the Rt. Hon. Sir John A. Macdonald.* Toronto, 1894.
_____. *The Day of Sir John Macdonald.* Toronto, 1920.
Pope, Maurice, ed. *Public Servant. The Memoirs of Sir Joseph Pope.* Toronto, 1960.
Preston, W.T.R. *My Generation of Politics and Politicians..* Toronto, 1927.
Ryerson, Egerton. *The Story of My Life.* Toronto, 1884.
Siegfried, André. *The Race Question in Canada.* Paris, 1906.
Skelton, O.D. *The Life and Times of Sir Alexander Tilloch Galt.* Toronto, 1920.
_____. *The Life and Times of Sir Wilfrid Laurier.* Toronto, 1921.
Smith, Goldwin. *The Bystander.* 1883.
_____. *Reminiscences.* New York, 1910.
Taylor, Fennings. *Are Legislatures Parliaments?* Montreal, 1879.
Turcotte, Louis P. *Le Canada sous l'Union 1841-1867.* Quebec, 1871-72.
Walker, G.C., ed. *Lady Dufferin's Canadian Journal 1872-1878.* Don Mills, 1969 (1891).
Wise, S.F., ed. *Sir Francis Bond Head: A Narrative.* Toronto, 1969 (1839).

E. *Constitutional Papers*

Hanham, J.J. *The Nineteenth Century Constitution.* Cambridge, 1969.
Kennedy, W.P.M. *Documents on the Canadian Constitution 1759-1915.* Toronto, 1918.

Williams, E. Neville. *The Eighteenth Century Constitution 1688-1815.* Cambridge, 1960.

F. *Miscellaneous*

Coté, J.O. *Political Appointments and Elections in the Province of Canada 1841-1865.* Ottawa, 1866.

Coté, M. Omer. *Political Appointments, Parliaments and The Judicial Bench 1867-1895.* Ottawa, 1896.

————. *Supplement: Political Appointments, Parliaments and the Judicial Bench 1896-1903.* Ottawa, 1903.

II. SECONDARY SOURCES

A. *Books (see note at beginning of bibliography)*

Armstrong, Christopher. *The Politics of Federalism: Ontario's Relations with the Federal Government 1867-1942.* Toronto, 1981.

Beck, J. Murray. *Pendulum of Power. Canada's Federal Elections.* Scarborough, ON. 1968.

————. *Joseph Howe.* 2 vols. Kingston and Montreal, 1983.

Berger, Carl. *The Writing of Canadian History: Aspects of English-Canadian History Writing 1900-1970.* Toronto, 1976.

Bliss, Michael. *A Living Profit: Studies in the Social History of Canadian Business 1884-1911.* Toronto, 1974.

Careless, J.M.S. *Brown of the Globe.* 2 vols. Toronto, 1959.

————, ed. *Pre-Confederation Premiers: Ontario Government Leaders 1841-1867.* Toronto, 1980.

Cornell, Paul G. *The Alignment of Political Groups in Canada 1841-1867.* Toronto, 1962.

Creighton, Donald G. *John A. Macdonald.* 2 vols. Toronto, 1955.

Desilets, André. *Hector-Louis Langevin: Un Père de la Confédération Canadienne 1826-1906.* Quebec, 1969.

Dumont, Fernand, and Jean-Paul Montminy, eds. *Le Pouvoir dans la Societé Canadienne-Francaise* Quebec, 1966.

Dales, John. *The Protective Tariff in Canada's Development.* Toronto, 1960.

Faucher, Albert. *Québec en Amérique au XIX siecle.* Montreal, 1973.

Firestone, O.J. *Canada's Economic Development 1867-1953.* London, 1958.

Garner, John. *The Franchise and Politics in British North America 1755-1867.* Toronto, 1969.

Gash, Norman. *Politics in the Age of Peel.* Oxford, 1953.

————. *Reaction and Reconstruction in English Politics 1832-1852.* Oxford, 1965.

Gibbons, Kenneth, and Donald Rowat. *Political Corruption in Canada.* Toronto, 1976.

Gibson, F.W., ed. *Cabinet Formation and Bicultural Relations.* Ottawa, 1970.

Guillet, Edwin C. *Early Life in Upper Canada.* Toronto, 1933.

Hamelin, Marcel. *The Political Ideas of the Prime Ministers of Canada.* Ottawa, 1969.

Harvey, A.D. *Britain in the Early Nineteenth Century.* New York, 1978.

Hodgetts, J.E. *Pioneer Public Service: An Administrative History of the United Canadas 1841-1867.* Toronto, 1955.

———, William McClosky, Reginald Whitaker, and V. Seymour Wilson. *The Biography of an Institution: The Civil Service Commission of Canada 1908-1967.* Montreal, 1972.

Hofstadter, Richard. *The Idea of a Party System: The Rise of Legitimate Opposition in the United States 1780-1840.* Berkeley, 1969.

LaPalombara, Joseph, ed. *Bureaucracy and Political Development.* Princeton, 1963.

———, and Myron Wiener, eds. *Political Parties and Political Revolution.* Princeton, 1966.

Mackay, R.A. *The Unreformed Senate of Canada.* Toronto, 1963.

McRae, Kenneth, ed. *Consociational Democracy. Political Accommodation in Segmented Societies.* Toronto 1974.

Martin, Ged. *The Durham Report and British Policy.* Cambridge, 1972.

Meekison, J. Peter. *Canadian Federalism.* Toronto, 1968.

Monet, Jacques. *The Last Cannon Shot: A Study of French-Canadian Nationalism 1837-1850.* Toronto, 1969.

Naylor, R.T. *The History of Canadian Business 1867-1914.* 2 vols. Toronto, 1975.

Neatby, H.B. *Laurier and a Liberal Quebec: A Study in Political Management.* Toronto, 1973.

Nelles, H.V. *The Politics of Development 1849-1941.* Toronto, 1974.

O'Gorman, Frank. *The Emergence of the British Two-Party System 1760-1832.* London, 1982.

Pacquet, Gilles, and Jean-Pierre Wallot. *Patronage et Pouvoir dans le Bas-Canada 1794-1812.* Quebec, 1973.

Plumb, J.H. *The Growth of Political Stability in England. 1675-1725.* London, 1967.

Pye, Lucien, and Sydney Verba, eds. *Political Culture and Political Development.* Princeton, 1965.

Read, Colin. *The Rising in Western Upper Canada 1837-1838.* Toronto, 1982.

Richards, Peter G. *Patronage in British Government.* London, 1963.

Saywell, John T. *The Office of Lieutenant-Governor.* Toronto, 1957.

Senior, Hereward. *Orangeism: The Canadian Phase.* Toronto, 1972.

Silver, A.I. *The French-Canadian Idea of Confederation 1864-1900.* Toronto, 1982.

Smiley, Donald. *The Canadian Political Nationality.* Toronto, 1967.

Swainson, Donald, ed. *Oliver Mowat's Ontario.* Toronto, 1972.

Sylvèstre, Guy, ed. *Structures Sociales du Canada Francais.* Quebec, 1966.

Thomson, Dale. *Alexander Mackenzie: Clear Grit.* Toronto, 1960.

Ward, Norman. *The Canadian House of Commons.* Toronto, 1950.

Wilson, George E. *Life of Robert Baldwin.* Toronto, 1933.

Zaslow, Morris, ed. *Profiles of a Province.* Toronto, 1967.

B. *Articles*

Beauen, Brian P.N. "Partisanship, Patronage, and the Press in Ontario, 1880-1914: Myths and Realities." *Canadian Historical Review (CHR).* 64 (1983):317-51.

Beer, D.R. "Sir Allan MacNab and the Adjutant-Generalship of Militia 1846-47." *Ontario History* 61 (1969).

Burke, Teresa A. "Mackenzie and His Cabinet." *CHR* 41 (1960): 128-48.

Cairns, Alan C. "The Electoral System and the Party System in Canada 1921-1965." *Canadian Journal of Political Science (CJPS)* 1 (1968): 55-79.

Clark, Lovell C. "The Conservative Party in the 1890's." Canadian Historical Association (CHA) *Report* (1961): 58-76.

Clark, S.D. "The Canadian Manufacturers Association." *Canadian Journal of Economics and Political Science (CJEPS)* 4 (1938): 505-23.

_____. "Sociology and Canadian Social History." *CJEPS* 5 (1939): 348-57.

Creighton, D.G. "Sir John A. Macdonald and Canadian Historians." *CHR* (1948): 1-13.

_____. "Sir John Macdonald and Kingston." CHA *Report* (1950): 72-80.

DaFoe, J.W. "Canada's Problems of Government." *CJEPS* 5 (1939): 285-99.

Dawson, R.M. "The Gerrymander of 1882." *CJEPS* 1 (1935): 197-221.

_____. "The Canadian Civil Service." *CJEPS* 2 (1936): 288-300.

Jones, Elwood. "Ephemeral Compromise. The Great Reform Convention Revisited." *Journal of Canadian Studies (JCS)* 3 (1968).

Lapierre, Laurier. "Joseph-Israel Tarte and the McGreevy-Langevin Scandal." CHA *Report* (1961): 47-57.

Lederle, John W. "The Liberal Convention of 1893." *CJEPS* 16 (1950): 42-52.

Livermore, J.D. "The Personal Agonies of Edward Blake." *CHR* 56 (1975).

McClokie, H.D. "The Modern Party State." *CJEPS* 15 (1949): 139-57.

Mackintosh, W.A. "Some Aspects of a Pioneer Economy." *CJEPS* 2 (1936): 457-63.

Ostry, Bernard. "Conservatives, Liberals and Labour in the 1870's." *CHR* 41 (1960): 93-127.

_____. "Conservatives, Liberals and Labour in the 1880's." *CJEPS* 27 (1961): 141-61.

Patterson, Graeme. "Whiggery, Nationality and the Upper Canadian Reform Tradition." *CHR* 56 (1975).

_____. "The Myths of Responsible Government and the Family Compact." *JCS* 12 (1977).

Pentland, H.C. "The Role of Capital in Canadian Economic Development before 1875." *CJEPS* 16 (1950): 457-75.

_____. "Observations on Canadian Development." *CJEPS* 19 (1953): 403-10.

Plumtree, A.F.W. "Political and Economic Development in the British Dominions." *CJEPS* 3 (1937): 489-507.

Reid, Escott. "The Rise of National Parties in Canada." CPSA *Proceedings* 4 (1932).

————. "The Saskatchewan Political Machine before 1929." *CJEPS* 2 (1936): 27-40.

Snell, J.G. "Frank Anglin Joins the Bench: a Study in Judicial Patronage." *Osgoode Hall Law Journal* 18 (1980): 664-673.

Stewart, Gordon T. "Political Patronage Under Macdonald and Laurier, 1878-1911." *The American Review of Canadian Studies* 10 (1980): 3-26.

————. "John A. Macdonald's Greatest Triumph." *CHR* 63 (1982): 3-33.

Swainson, Donald "Business and Politics: the Career of John Willoughby Crawford." *Ontario History* 61 (1969): 225-36.

Underhill, F.H. "The Concept of National Interest." *CJEPS* 1 (1935): 396-408.

————. "The Development of National Parties in Canada." *CHR* 16 (1935): 367-87.

————. "The Canadian Party System in Transition." *CJEPS* 9 (1943): 300-313.

Ward, Norman. "Parliamentary Representation in Canada 1872-1945." *CJEPS* 13 (1947): 447-64.

————. "The Basis of Representation in the House of Commons." *CJEPS* 15 (1949): 477-94.

————. "Electoral Corruption and Controverted Elections." *CJEPS* 15 (1949): 74-86.

————. "Responsible Government: an Introduction." *JCS* 14 (1979).

Young, Brian. "The Defeat of Georges E. Cartier in Montreal East in 1872." *CHR* 51 (1970): 386-406.

INDEX

Adams, John, 17

American Revolution: impact of on concepts of power and government, 2-3, 9-10; and emergence of republican institutions, 18-19

Anglican Church. **See** Church of England

Armstrong, Christopher (historian), on federal/provincial relations in 19th century, 84

Arthur, Sir George (Lieutenant-Governor of Upper Canada, 1838-41), forecasts constitutional course in Union, 46

Bagehot, Walter, on role of deference in Victorian Britain, 55

Bailyn, Bernard (historian), on origins of American politics, 1-2

Baldwin, Robert: characterized by Lord Elgin, 28; his "court" concept of reform, 28, 44

Bank of England, 13

Beck, J. Murray (political scientist), on Joseph Howe and patronage, 88

Bell, David (political scientist), application of Hartzian model to Canada, 4-5

Berger, Carl (historian), on nature of Canadian history writing, 8

Birmingham, Robert, and QC appointments in Ontario, 78

Blackstone, William, on Crown and Parliament in Britain, 17

Blake, Edward, attitude towards patronage politics, 71-73

Boer War, 74

Bonenfant, Jean-Charles (historian), on politics and social structure in Quebec, 86

Borden, Robert Laird, attitude of, towards patronage, 89

Bouchette, M. Errol, on French Canadians and responsible government, 51

Boulton, Henry, proposes Tory reform of legislative council, 61

British Columbia, 87

Brown, George: role of, in party development, 65; contrasted with Macdonald, 71

Campbell, Alexander, role of, in Conservative party, 68

Canada Act (1791), 3, 9. **See also** constitution of 1791

Careless, J.M.S. (historian), on constitution in early Union, 48

Cartier, George-Etienne, role of, in early Conservative party, 64-65

Cassells, C.T., investigation by, of Department of Marine and Fisheries, 76-77

Castlereagh, Viscount, 25

Catholic Church: role of, in post-conquest Quebec, 21; role of, in politics, 62-63

Chamberlin, Brown, 63

Charles II, 11

Chateau Clique, 30-31, 33

Church of England: its place in England after 1688, 11; fate of, in the Canadas, 40-41; intended role of, in 1791, 24

Civil Service Act (1868), ineffectiveness of, 75-76

Civil Service Commission (1907-08), its assessment of patronage after 1867, 76-78

Clark, S.D. (sociologist), on Canadian middle classes, 87

Collins, J.E., on development of Conservative party, 68

Colonial Gazette, assessment of Governor Metcalfe, 48